WILLIAM USSELINX
AVTEVR VAN WESTINDISH COMPAGNIE
AET SVAE 60 AO 1637

WILLIAM WSSELINX
Avtevr van Westindise Compangi
Aet. Svae 69. Ao. 1637

THE DUTCH FOUNDING
OF NEW YORK

BY

THOMAS A. JANVIER

AUTHOR OF "IN OLD NEW YORK"
"THE CHRISTMAS KALENDS OF PROVENCE" ETC.

ILLUSTRATED

NEW YORK AND LONDON
HARPER & BROTHERS PUBLISHERS
1903

ILLUSTRATIONS

PAGE

W. WSSELINX. (Avtevr van Westindise Compangi Aet. Svae 69. Ao. 1637) . *Frontispiece*

MAP OF NEW NETHERLAND. CIRCA 1616 . *facing*   20

THE WEST INDIA COMPANY'S HOUSE, HAARLEMMER STRAAT, AMSTERDAM. 1623–1647 . *facing*   30

THE WEST INDIA COMPANY'S WAREHOUSE AS SEEN FROM THE OUDE SCHANS, AMSTERDAM. —(Built in the year 1641. Used as the Company's meeting-place in the years 1647–1674) . . . . *facing*   46

EARLIEST KNOWN VIEW OF NEW AMSTERDAM. CIRCA 1630.—Reversed (following Mr. J. H. Innes) from Joost Hartger's *Beschrijvingh van Virginia, Nieuw Nederlandt, etc.* . . . *facing*   66

VIEW OF NEW AMSTERDAM. CIRCA 1650. SHOWING THE CAPSKE ROCKS, NOW COVERED BY BATTERY PARK.—(From the *Beschrijvingh van Amerika* of Arnoldus Montanus. Amsterdam, 1671) . . . . *facing*   84

THE TOWN HOUSE (STADT HUYS), NEW YORK, 1679.—(Redrawn from the Dankers and Sluyter drawing. See *Memoirs of the Long Island Historical Society*, vol. i.) . . . . . *facing*   96

iii

ILLUSTRATIONS

PAGE

THE VISSCHER MAP, WITH A VIEW OF NEW AM-
STERDAM DRAWN BEFORE THE YEAR 1653 *facing* 112

THE WATER GATE, FOOT OF WALL STREET, 1679.
—(Redrawn from the Dankers and Sluyter
drawing. See *Memoirs of the Long Island
Historical Society*, vol. i.) . . . . . *facing* 122

THE ALLAERDT VIEW OF NEW YORK. CIRCA
1668.—(From the map of Reinier and Josua
Ottens) . . . . *facing* 138

VIEW OF NEW YORK FROM BROOKLYN HEIGHTS,
1679. — (From the Dankers and Sluyter
drawing) . . . . *facing* 166

" THE DUKE'S PLAN," 1661–1664. (Photographed
for this work from the original in the British
Museum. Showing New Amsterdam in the
year that it became New York) . . . *facing* 188

THE DUTCH FOUNDING
OF NEW YORK

THE DUTCH FOUNDING
OF NEW YORK

I

ARTFUL fiction being more convinc-
ing than artless fact, it is not likely
that the highly untruthful impression of
the Dutch colonists of Manhattan given
by Washington Irving ever will be ef-
faced. Very subtly mendacious is Irving's delightful *History of New York from
the Beginning of the World to the End of
the Dutch Dynasty.* Bearing in mind the
time when he wrote — before Mr. Brodhead had performed the great work of

I

collecting in Europe the documents re-
lating to our colonial history, and while
the records of the city and of the State
still were in confusion—his general truth
to the letter is surprising. But precisely
because of his truth to the letter are his
readers misled by his untruth to the
spirit. Over the facts which he was at
such pains to gather and to assemble, he
has cast everywhere the glamour of a be-
littling farcical romance: with the result
that his humorous conception of our an-
cestral Dutch colony peopled by a sleepy
tobacco-loving and schnapps-loving race
stands in the place of the real colony
peopled by hard-headed and hard-hitting
men.

Irving's fancy undoubtedly is kindlier
than the plain truth. They were a rough
lot, those Dutchmen who settled here in
Manhattan nearly three hundred years

2

ago; and they did not—the phrase is from
our own frontier vocabulary—come here
for their health. As has happened in the
case of much later outpost settlements
on this continent, they cheated the savages whom they found in residence, and
most cruelly oppressed them. Also, on
occasion, they cheated one another; out
of which habit, as is shown by the verbose
records of their little courts, arose much
petty litigation of a snarling sort among
themselves. In a larger and more impersonal fashion, they consistently cheated the revenue laws of the colony; and
with a fine equanimity they broke any
other laws which happened to get in their
way—a line of conduct that is not to be
condemned sweepingly, however, because
most of the revenue laws of the colony,
and many of its general laws, were unjust
intrinsically and were administered in a

3

manner that gave to those who evaded or
who broke them a good deal in the way of
colorable excuse. In a word, our Dutch
ancestors who founded this city had the
vices of their kind enlarged by the vices
of their time. But, also, they had certain virtues—unmentioned by Irving—
which in their time were, and in our time
still are, respectable. With all their shortcomings, they were tough and they were
sturdy and they were as plucky as men
could be. Of the easy-going somnolent
habit that Irving has fastened upon them
as their dominant characteristic there is
not to be found in the records the slight-
est trace. I am satisfied that that characteristic did not exist.

Certainly, there was no suggestion of
somnolence in the promptness with which
the Dutch followed up Hudson's practical
discovery of the river that now bears his

4

name. Hudson's immediate backers, to
be sure, the members of the Dutch East
India Company, took no action in the
premises. They had sent him out to find
a northerly passage to the Indies—and
that he had not found. What he had
found was of no use to them. The region
drained by his great river was outside the
limits of their charter; and trade with it
did not promise—though promising much
—returns at all comparable with those
which were pouring in upon them from
their spice-trade with the East. Therefore, his voyage having been a mere waste
of their money, they charged off the cost
of it to profit and loss and so closed the
account—while the great navigator, being seized by his own government out
of the Dutch service, went off to sea
again: on that final quest of his for the
impossible passage to the east by the

5

north that ended in his death in Hudson's Bay.

But when Hudson's report of the fur-yielding country that he had found was made public in Holland certain other of the Dutch merchants pricked up their ears. These were the traders who carried European and Eastern goods to Russia and there bartered them for Muscovy furs: a commerce that had its beginning toward the end of the sixteenth century, and that was greatly stimulated by certain concessions granted by the Czar to the Dutch in the year 1604. Those concessions provided, in effect, that goods might be imported into Russia, and that goods to an equal value might be exported thence, on the payment of landing and loading duties of two and a half per cent., while on exports above the value of imports a farther duty of five per cent. was

6

laid: a tariff system which, for those times, was at once so liberal and so simple that it drew to Archangel a fleet of from sixty to eighty Dutch ships a year.

But Hudson's exposition of the fur-trade possible in America made a still better showing. In dealing with ingenuous savages, unhampered by a government of any sort whatever, there would be no duties to pay on either imports or exports; and instead of being compelled to give value for value—a custom that all traders of all times have resented—a shipload of furs could be had for the insignificant outlay of a few jerry-made hatchets and some odds and ends of beads. (It is but just to the Netherlanders to add that, in the passing of the centuries, they have lost nothing of their acuteness in such matters: as is evidenced by their ability to get and to keep the weather-gauge of

7

the unlucky savages of the Congo Protectorate to-day.) And so, in the summer of 1610, certain merchants of Amsterdam —suffering no grass to grow under their feet—despatched to the island of Manhattan a vessel loaded with "a cargo of goods suitable for traffic with the Indians": and no doubt but it was a precious lot of rubbish that they put on board!

I am sorry to say that the name of that first trading-ship sent to this port remains unknown. But the fact of her sailing is established, as is also the fact that her crew in part was made up of men who had sailed with Hudson in the *Half Moon*. Mr. Brodhead is of the opinion that she was commanded by Hudson's Dutch mate; and he cites the tradition that the Hollanders who came again to this island, and the Indians living here,

were "much rejoiced at seeing each
other ": a cordiality which—however reasonable it might have been on the side of
the Dutch—showed that the savages had
no endowment of prophetic instinct to
warn them that the stars in their courses
were fighting against them, and that then
was the beginning of their end.

For my present purposes it suffices to
say that the briskness with which that
first trading voyage was undertaken and
accomplished strikes the key-note of
Dutch character. Keenness and alert-
ness—not the drowsiness upon which
Irving so harps in his persistent pleasantries—were the personal and national
characteristics of the people who founded
this city; and who founded it, we must
remember, in the very thick of their
glorious fight for freedom with what then
was the first sea power of the world.

Those qualities clearly were in evidence in their despatch to Manhattan—almost on the instant that Hudson's report of his discovery was made public—of that little nameless merchantman: with the coming of which into this harbor, solely as a trader, the commerce of the port of New York began.

II

THERE was a nice touch of prophetic
fitness in the fact that the very first
product of skilled labor on our island was
a ship; and a still nicer touch—since the
commercial supremacy of our city was
assured at the outset by its combined
command of salt-water and of fresh-water
navigation—in the farther fact that that
ship was large enough to venture out
upon the ocean, and yet was small enough
to work her way far into the interior of
the continent: up the channels of the
thirteen rivers which fall into, or which
have their outlet through, New York Bay.
And, also, I like to fancy that the spirit
of prophecy was upon the Dutch builders

of that heroically great little vessel when they named her the *Onrust:* because, assuredly, the word " Restless "—in its sense of untiring energy—at once describes the most essential characteristic of, and is the most fit motto for, the city of New York. Indeed, I wish that this early venture in ship-building had been remembered when our civic arms were granted to us; and that then—instead of our beaver and of our later-added wind-mill sails and flour-barrels, full of meaning though those charges are—we had been given a ship for our device, and with it for our motto the pregnant word: "Onrust."

Our little first ship—built almost in the glowing moment of the city's founding—was a child of disaster; but all the more for that reason, I think, was the making of her heroic. Following quickly

in the wake of the little nameless merchantman, other ships were sent to the
river Mauritius—as they were beginning
to call it in honor of their Stadtholder—to
win a share of the profits in the newly-
opened trade. From Amsterdam were
sent the *Fortune*, commanded by Hendrick Christiansen, and the *Tiger*, commanded by Adrien Block; and another
ship, also called the *Fortune*, commanded
by Cornelis Jacobsen, was sent out from
Hoorn. By the year 1613 half a dozen
voyages had been made; and by that time,
also, there was some sort of a little trading-post here: a group of huts, possibly
stockaded, which stood where the Fort
stood later and where the irrational walls
of the new custom-house are rising now.

The disaster to which the building of
the *Onrust* was due was the burning of
Block's ship, the *Tiger*, just as he was

13

making ready to return in her to Holland
—in the autumn of the year 1613. Had
Block and his men been of a ruminative
habit—the habit that Irving has ascribed
to the Dutch generally—they would have
meditated the winter through, with their
hands in their pockets, upon the disaster
that had overtaken them. What they
actually did was to set to work instantly
to build another vessel. Presumably they
saved from the burned *Tiger* what little
iron - work they needed (ships in those
days were pegged together with wooden
pins, which fact accounts for their coming apart so easily and leaking so pro-
digiously), and for ship-timber there was
not need to go farther up town—as we
should say nowadays — than Rector
Street; very likely there was not need
to go so far. And so they buckled down
to their work, and by the spring-time of

the year 1614 the *Onrust* was finished
and launched: a yacht, as she was classed,
of forty-four feet six inches keel; eleven
feet six inches beam; and of "about eight
lasts burthen"—that is to say, of about
sixteen tons. The Dutch are not a de-
monstrative race—but I fancy that there
was cheering on this island on the day
that the *Onrust* slid down the ways!

There is good ground for believing that
the ship-yard in which Block and his men
worked was close by the present meeting
place of Pearl and Broad streets, on the
bank of the creek that then flowed where
Broad Street now is. It is my very earnest hope that a monument may be set
up there to commemorate that great
building of our little first ship: the ancestor of all the ships which have been
built on this island in the now nearly completed three centuries since she took the

15

water; the ancestor of all the ships which will be built on this island in all the centuries to come. And I am the more eager to see my monument erected because at this very time precisely the site for it is being prepared. The purchase of Fraunces's Tavern, for permanent preservation, includes the purchase of a half-block of land at Pearl and Broad streets —whence the modern houses are to be removed, that in their place may be laid out a little park. Possibly the *Onrust* was built on the very piece of land thus to be vacated; almost certainly she was built not a stone's cast from its borders. In that park, therefore, the monument to New York's first ship must stand.

As the direct result of the building of the *Onrust* the Dutch field of American discovery and possession materially was enlarged. Block sailed away in her, in the

16

sunshine of that long-past spring-time, to explore the bays and rivers to the eastward—"into which the larger ships of the Dutch traders had not ventured." He laid his course boldly through Hell Gate —it is probable that the *Onrust* was the first sailing vessel to make that perilous passage — and, going onward through Long Island Sound, crossed Narragansett Bay and Buzzard's Bay, coasted Cape Cod, and made his highest northing in "Pye Bay, as it is called by some of our navigators, in latitude 42° 30′, to which the limits of New Netherland extend." As he returned southward he fell in with the *Fortune*, homeward bound from Manhattan, and went back in her to Holland to report upon the new countries which he had found—leaving the *Onrust* to make farther voyages of discovery under the command of Cornelis Hendricksen.

Block's claim that Pye Bay (in mercy to summer residents upon the North Shore of Massachusetts, we call it Nahant Bay now) marked the limits of New Netherland to the northward was one of those liberal assertions common to the explorers of his day. That claim clashed with claims under English grants, and while it was asserted it was not maintained. But the Dutch did claim resolutely, in their subsequent wranglings with the English, as far north as the Fresh Water —that is to say, the Connecticut river: on the ground that Block was the first European to enter that river, and that the Dutch planted the first European colony upon its banks. On like grounds they claimed, and for a long while held without dispute, the whole of Long Island. Broadly speaking, therefore, the building of the *Onrust* and the voyages made in her resulted in bringing within the Dutch "sphere of influence," as we should phrase it nowadays, both shores of Long Island Sound.

The official record of what the *Onrust* accomplished, and of what came of it, was spread upon the minutes of the States General (August 18, 1616) in these words: "Cornelis Henricxs⁸, Skipper, appears before the Assembly, assisted by Notary Carel van Geldre, on behalf of Gerrit Jacob Witssen, Burgomaster at Amsterdam, Jonas Witssen, Lambrecht van Tweenhuyzen, Paulus Pelgrom *cum suis*, Directors of New Netherland, extending from forty to five - and - forty degrees, situate in America between New France and Virginia, rendering a Report of the second Voyage, of the manner in which the aforesaid Skipper hath found and discovered a certain country, bay, and three rivers [the Housatonic, Connecticut, and Pequod, or Thames] lying between the thirty-eighth and fortieth degree of Latitude (as is more fully to be seen by the Figurative Map) in a small yacht of about eight Lasts, named the *Onrust*. Which little yacht they caused to be built in the aforesaid Country, where they employed the said Skipper in looking for new countries, havens, bays, rivers etc. Requesting the privilege to trade exclusively to the aforesaid countries for the term of four years, according to their High Mightiness's placard issued in March 1614. It is resolved, before determining herein, that the Comparants shall be ordered to render and to transmit in writing the Report that they have made."

III

"THEIR High Mightiness's placard," above cited, was an epoch-making document. It had its origin in a joint resolution of the states of Holland and West Vriesland taken March 20, 1614, "on the Remonstrance of divers merchants wishing to discover new unknown rivers countries and places not sought for (nor resorted to) heretofore from these parts"; and it declared that "whoever shall resort to and discover such new lands and places shall alone be privileged to make four voyages to such lands and places from these countries, exclusive of every other person, until the aforesaid four voyages shall have been completed."

21

To make the resolution effective, it was sent up to be confirmed by the Assembly of the United Provinces at The Hague; and there, evidently, it had strong backers who were in a hurry. Their High Mightinesses were not given to acting precipitately. Quite the contrary. But on that occasion—as the result, we reasonably may assume, of very lively lobbying on the part of a delegation sent to The Hague from Amsterdam—the resolution of the states of Holland and West Vriesland was "railroaded" at such a rate that in a single week the Assembly had embodied it (March 27th) in a placard, or proclamation, which gave it the authority of a national law. As the making of Manhattan was the outcome of the local resolution and of the general proclamation which gave it effective force, a pleasing parallel may be drawn between this

22

piece of brisk legislation and other pieces
of brisk legislation in later times; indeed,
it is not too much to assert that the precedent then was established of sending
lobbying delegations from New York to
Albany—and I see no reason for doubt-
ing that The Hague lobby was run then
very much as the Albany lobby is run
now. Customs and clothes change from
one century to another; but it is well to
remember (Borbonius and his *omnia mu-
tantur* to the contrary notwithstanding)
that the men inside of the customs and
the clothes do not change much from age
to age.

Without going deeper into this matter
of ethics, it suffices here to state that the
placard issued by the States General gave
the Amsterdam ring what it wanted—
but with a commendably greater dignity
of expression than usually is found in the

23

legislative acts affecting " cities of the first class" which issue from Albany to-day. The charging points of that famous placard are as follows: " Whereas, we understand that it would be honourable serviceable and profitable to this Country, and for the promotion of its prosperity, as well as for the maintenance of seafaring people, that the good Inhabitants should be excited and encouraged to employ and to occupy themselves in seeking out and discovering Passages, Havens, Countries, and Places that have not before now been discovered nor frequented; and being informed by some Traders that they intend, with God's merciful help, by diligence labour danger and expense, to employ themselves thereat, as they expect to derive a handsome profit therefrom, if it pleased Us to privilege charter and favour them that they alone might

24

resort and sail to and frequent the passages havens countries and places to be
by them newly found and discovered for
six voyages, as a compensation for their
outlays trouble and risk. . . . Therefore:
We, having duly weighed the aforesaid
matter, and finding, as hereinbefore
stated, the said undertaking to be laud-
able honourable and serviceable for the
prosperity of the United Provinces, and
wishing that the experiment be free and
open to all and every of the inhabitants
of this country . . . do hereby grant and
consent that whosoever from now hence-
forward shall discover any new Passages
Havens Countries or Places shall alone
resort to the same or cause them to be
frequented for four voyages, without any
other person directly or indirectly sailing
frequenting or resorting from the United
Netherlands to the said newly discovered

and found passages havens countries or
places until the first discoverer and finder shall have made, or caused to be made,
the said four voyages: on pain of confiscation of the goods and ships wherewith
the contrary attempt shall be made, and
a fine of Fifty thousand Netherland Duc-
ats, to the profit of the aforesaid finder
or discoverer."

It would seem from the foregoing that
the Amsterdam men asked for six voyages
and were granted four: even as at Albany
"a strike" nowadays is so made that the
Assembly may manifest a fine faithful-
ness to the public interests by cutting
it down handsomely—and still give the
"strikers" all they want. Again I may
observe that in this energetic piece of
legislation — obviously rushed through
that older Assembly by powerful private
interest—there is no very pointed mani-

26

festation of the Dutch sleepiness upon which Irving so freely descants.

Indeed, as I have already stated, and as I shall state more at length presently, the Dutch showed a most lively eagerness during the years immediately following Hudson's discovery to seize upon and to develop the North American trade. Broadly, they sought to capture that trade before it fell into the hands of other nations. Narrowly, they sought to wrest it from one another—as may be seen in the fierce contention for trading privileges which went on among themselves. Petitions and counter-petitions for trading rights pestered the local assemblies of the states and the States General. One large company was formed to take, and for a time did take, the whole of the American contract. There was a constant wrangling that disturbed the land. Partly to quiet that wrangling, but more to serve high national interests, measures at last were taken which put an end to all rivalries (other than with outsiders) by creating a single powerful corporation to which was granted all trading right to America.

IV

VERY great principles of religion and
of state, along with other principles
of a strictly commonplace selfish sort, lay
at the root of the founding of the Dutch
West India Company. In a grand way,
that Company was intended to win freedom for the Netherlands by smashing the
power of Spain. In a less grand way—
but in a way that never was lost sight of
—it was intended to line the pockets of
the practical patriots who were its stock-
holders. On its larger lines, as an instrument of justice, and incidentally as an
instrument of personal and political revenge, it was to a great extent a success.
On its smaller lines, as a commercial in-

vestment, it was a ruinous failure. We of New York are none the better for its success, and we distinctly are the worse for its failure. That failure gave this city a bad start.

William Usselincx, the originator of the Company, and for thirty years its most persistent promoter, was one of the half million or so of Protestant Belgians who were driven to take refuge in Holland by Spanish persecution. As an Antwerp merchant, under Spanish rule, he had traded to America; and so had come to know that the colonies whence Spain drew her main revenues were at once her strength and her weakness. He realized that those colonies, widely scattered and individually ill-defended, were secure only because they were not attacked; and he farther realized that even a small naval force, resolutely handled, could give a

good account of the treasure-fleets which sailed annually from America to Spain. His simple plan, developed from those conditions,.was to seize and to sack the richer cities of the Spanish islands and the Spanish main, and to capture such plate-ships as could be caught conveniently upon the sea—with the immediate result of a very satisfactory return in cash from his sackings and capturings, and with an ultimate result of a greater and more far-reaching sort. On that larger side was patriotism. His great purpose was to cripple Spain by seizing her revenues at their source, and still farther to cripple her by breaking her line of communication with that source: both by the actual capture of her treasure-laden ships, and by the threat of capture that would make Spanish ship-masters fearful of their voyage. The threat was a potent one. In

our own day, when the *Alabama* was
afloat, we have seen what such a threat,
backed by only a ship or two, will do to
wreck the commerce of a nation by driv-
ing its vessels to the shelter of foreign
flags. In those large days of hard fighting refuge under a foreign flag was a
thing unknown. Spain had no choice but
to stand up and take Dutch punishment
until—and that was intended to be the
glorious ending of the struggle — she
should be so weakened that her hold
upon the Netherlands could be broken
for good and all.

It was about the year 1592 that Usselincx broached his heroic project for or-
ganizing that private military corporation
which anticipated by almost precisely
three centuries Mr. Stockton's "Great
War Syndicate": an association of financiers who, in a strictly business way, were

to expel the Spaniards from the Netherlands—and who were to net upon the
transaction a profit of from fifty to one
hundred per cent. Also, it was on business lines that his project was opposed—
but with a mingling in the opposition of
considerations of classes and of creeds.
The destruction by the Spaniards of the
commerce of Antwerp had thrown a large
part of that commerce to Rotterdam and
Amsterdam. It was asking a good deal,
therefore, to ask the Dutch to take a
hand in a venture that would bring them
to grips with the strongest State in the
world; and that would have for its outcome, if successful, the return of the
Belgian refugees in triumph to their own
country to re-establish — at the cost of
their Dutch allies—their lost trade on the
Scheldt. John of Barneveldt, as a statesman—perhaps as a somewhat narrow-

minded statesman—opposed the Belgian
plan. Behind him were the town aris-
tocracies of birth and of wealth, the
advocates of republicanism, the Arminians. The Belgians had for allies the
lower classes in the towns of Holland, the
monarchists, the strict Calvinists, and for
a rallying centre the House of Orange—
the head of which great House, taking a
strictly personal interest in the matter,
played always and only for his own hand.

The two great parties then formed lasted intact until the French Revolution,
and are not extinct even now. For
thirty years the fight between them—
broadly on the Belgian matter, but with
many side issues—was waged vigorously.
In the first acute stage of the struggle,
1607–1609, the main issues were war or
truce or peace with Spain—and the threat
implied by Usselincx's project had much

34

to do with compelling Spain to accept
the humiliating twelve years' truce that
was signed in the year 1609. In the
second acute stage, 1617–1619, the main
issue was theological: the fight for supremacy between the Calvinists and the
Arminians. That fight ended, on May
13, 1619, with the execution of Barneveldt. Then Usselincx's plan was taken
up in good earnest: with the result that
things began to move forward briskly
toward the founding of New York.

I confess that there is a suggestion of
anticlimax in treating as mere incidents
of that great struggle the wrecking of
the power of Spain and the winning of
freedom for the United Netherlands; and
as its culmination nothing more stirring
than the establishment of a fur-traders'
camp on a lonely islet nooked in the
waters of an almost unknown land. But

I protest that, for my present purposes, the most important result which flowed from the rise of the Dutch Republic precisely was the establishment of that fur-traders' camp.

V

JUST the same human nature that still is in use showed itself in the fight that went on in the Low Countries during those strenuous thirty years. That much is made clear by the records of the states of Holland and of West Vriesland—where the Belgian party was strongest—and by the records of the States General. But the spicy personal details of the conflict, being hid in the phrases "divers merchants" and "divers traders," are lost.

On June 21, 1614, when the light sparring of the second round was beginning, a petition of "divers traders of these provinces" was presented to the States General praying for power to form

"a general Company for the West Indies,
the coast of Africa, and through the
Straits of Magellan." The petition was
ordered to lie over for four weeks, to the
end that "their High Mightinesses may
thoroughly examine the matter"; but its
opponents—by means which were not recorded in the minutes—managed to keep
it in committee for more than two months.
It did come up again, however, on the
25th of August; and so vigorously that
the Assembly voted "that the business
of forming a general West India Company shall be undertaken to-morrow
morning." Again the opposition got in
some fine work—and the business was not
undertaken on that "to-morrow morning" of nearly three hundred years ago.
It was adjourned until September 2d. On
that day the two parties came to a clinch
—that ended for the Belgian party in a

clean fall. During the morning the Belgians clearly had the lead, and the Assembly resolved "that the affair of the West India Company shall be continued this afternoon." But it wasn't—and before the West India Company was founded that momentary stoppage had stretched out into nine years. Very interesting would be the record—if it existed, and if we could get at it—of what happened that day at The Hague after the morning session of the Assembly stood adjourned! Having no record to go by, we can only make guesses: being guided a little in our guessing by knowledge of what has happened at Albany, between two sessions of another Assembly, in later times.

A little light is thrown on the situation by an act passed (September 27, 1614) by the states of Holland and West Vriesland: in which is the pointed suggestion that under cover of a general company "some may secretly endeavor to pursue trade to Guinea . . . in case the trade to other countries should . . . happen to fail, to be interrupted, or to cease." Possibly, then, the Dutch slave - traders had a hand in "knifing" the bill that day. Some measures in our own Congress were "knifed" by the slave-holding interest much less than three centuries ago. Also, it is fair to assume that the promoters of the New Netherland Company had much to do with the "knifing." Certainly, that Company was chartered only a little more than a month after the West India Company went by the board.

Among the members of the New Netherland Company were Hans Hongers, Paulus Pelgrom, and Lambrecht van Tweenhuysen, owners of the ships *Tiger* and *Fortune*—and therefore the owners of the yacht *Onrust:* and the major claim on which they rested their request for special trading privileges was their right to benefit from the discoveries that had resulted from the little yacht's voyage. To that Company the States General granted a charter (October 11, 1614) which gave an exclusive right " to resort to, or cause to be frequented, the afore-said newly discovered countries situate in America between New France and Virginia, the sea coasts whereof lie in the Latitude of from forty to forty five degrees, now named New Netherland, as is to be seen by a Figurative Map hereunto annexed; and that for four Voyages within the term of three years, commencing the first January 1615 next coming, or sooner."

In that document the name "New Netherland" first was used officially; and

41

was used, to quote Mr. Brodhead, to designate the "unoccupied regions of America lying between Virginia and Canada by a name which they continued to bear for half a century—until, in the fullness of time, right gave way to power and the Dutch colony of New Netherland became the English province of New York."

The question of title that Mr. Brodhead raises in this loose statement of fact is far too large a question to be dealt with here. But it is only fair to add that his hot contention that the Dutch had a just right to their North American holding is denied with equal heat by a Dutch authority. The peppery Dr. Asher — in his life of Hudson, prepared for the Hakluyt Society —disposes of the claims of his own countrymen in these words: "The [Dutch] title itself was little better than a shadow.

It was entirely founded on the boldest, the most obstinate, and the most extensive act of 'squatting' recorded in colonial history. The territory called New Netherland, which the West India Company claimed on account of Hudson's discovery, belonged by the best possible right to England. It formed part of a vast tract of country, the coast of which had been first discovered by English ships, on which settlements had been formed by English colonists, and which had been publicly claimed by England, and granted to an English company before Hudson ever set foot on American ground. But the wilds and wastes of primeval forests were thought of so little value that the Dutch were for many years allowed to encroach upon English rights, without more than passing remonstrance of the British government."

43

It is my duty to state the clashing opinions of these two fiery historians; but I have not the effrontery to discuss the question on which, so signally, they are at odds. Nor is discussion necessary. Most happily, that once burning question was quieted by the Treaty of Breda (1667) and has been a dead issue for more than two hundred years.

In the end, as I have written, Usselincx and the Belgians won through. When John of Barneveldt's head ceased to be associated with his body—the equities of that detachment need not here be discussed—opposition to the founding of the West India Company came to an end. The actual establishment of the Company had to be postponed until the expiration of the truce with Spain; but matters immediately were set in train for it, and in the year 1621, upon the renewal of hostilities, the act of incorporation (June 3d) was passed.

Under the terms of the charter—which, as Mr. Brodhead puts it, "created a sort of marine principality with sovereign rights on foreign shores"—the Company was granted exclusive rights to trade on the coasts of Africa between the Tropic of Cancer and the Cape of Good Hope; to the West Indies; and to the coast of America between New Foundland and the Straits of Magellan: with power to make treaties, to found colonies within those limits, to appoint governors over such colonies, to administer justice in them, and to raise a military force for their defence. Farther, the States General engaged to defend the Company against every person in free navigation and traffic; to "assist" it with a grant of a million guilders; and to give it sixteen warships—that the Company was to man and to equip, and to match by raising an equal naval force of its own: the whole fleet to be under the command of an admiral whom the States General should name. Also, the States General reserved the right to confirm or to reject the governors nominated by the Company, and to exercise a general control of its affairs.

Thus, at last, the Dutch West India Company was launched. Had Irving touched upon its history he probably would have attributed the long delay to Dutch sleepiness; and would have given us many neatly-turned pleasantries about the number of pipes smoked drowsily, and about the drowsy talk that went on for thirty years between those stolid Dutch statesmen and those stolid Dutch financiers—all of which would have been

West Indis Huys

THE WEST INDIA COMPANY'S WAREHOUSE AS SEEN FROM THE OUDE SCHANS, AMSTERDAM

(Built in the year 1641. Used as the Co...

vastly amusing, but would have left something on the side of fact to be desired.

There was substantial cause for that
long delay. In addition to the great
problems of statecraft that had to be
dealt with, the Dutch were dealing with
a new great project on new great lines.
Their nearest approach to a precedent
was the East India Company: of which
the primary purpose—as trade went and
as peace was understood in those days—
was peaceful trade. The primary purpose of the West India Company was
war. Its main dividends were expected
to come from, and eventually did come
from, the capture of Spanish treasure.
But provision had to be made for earning money in between whiles—during the
close season for treasure-hunting — by
employing its armed fleet in ordinary
trade: in carrying cargoes of slaves and

47

peltries and other general merchandise
of the times. And at every turn conflicting interests, political and commercial, had to be reconciled and brought
into line. Nowadays a half-dozen corporation lawyers would get together and
would organize such a company in a fortnight; and in another fortnight—under
the New Jersey general corporation act
—it would have its charter and would be
established as a going concern. But we
do these things quickly now—being also
freed from the trammels of state policy
—because we have precedents in abun-
dance to work by, and because we have
the tools to work with (I use the phrase
with a broad impersonality) lying ready
to our hands. To take a strictly legal
parallel: any little seventeenth-century
English conveyancer was able to get the
weather-gauge of the Statute of Uses after

Orlando Bridgman had shown him how.
Yet sleepiness—whatever may be said of
its slowness—never has been suggested
as a distinguishing characteristic of the
seventeenth - century English bar. Nor
were the Dutch of that century sleepy.
They were very wide awake indeed.

One other point in the making of the
West India Company I must touch upon.
With the sincere immodesty that is not
the least marked of our civic traits, we
of New York are accustomed to believe
that that Company was organized and
chartered mainly for the purpose of ex-
ploiting our own New Netherland. Actually, the part that our little island (and
its dependent continent) had in that large
piece of statecraft was microscopic: as
we realize when we consider the great
elements—rival trade interests, contend-
ing factions, warring creeds—which were

combined in it under the strangely blended pressure of sordid selfishness and lofty
patriotism and hot revenge. Looked at
in that way, there is nothing in the history of the Company to stir our vanity.
But looked at in another way, even our
vanity has its consolations. Although the
splendid part that the Company took in
fighting to a glorious finish the glorious
fight that Holland put up with Spain is
not forgotten, its share of honor in a way
is lost: being merged into, and almost
indistinguishably blended with, the national honor which the Dutch won by a
victory that instantly benefited, and that
still continues to benefit, the whole civ-
ilized world. But the Company shared
with no one the glory of planting the city
of New Amsterdam, that in time's fulness
was to be the city of New York—nor had
it, I venture incidentally to assert, the

least notion that out of that trifling colonial venture any glory ever would come. Yet that most minor of all its accomplishments is precisely the accomplishment that has kept green its memory; that will continue to keep green its memory as long as New York endures.

I hasten to add that we owe the Company no thanks. What it did for the making of our city was done badly—and the very founding of it was barely more than a mere by-blow of chance. In point of fact, the nearest approach to naming New Netherland in the Company's charter was the permissive clause referring to the colonization of "fruitful and unsettled lands." At least, the description is recognizable. While Manhattan no longer is unsettled, it certainly is fruitful still.

VI

EVEN before the West India Company was organized the germ of the
destruction of Dutch rule in North America had taken form.   In November 1620
the patent had passed the Great Seal by
which King James granted to the Plymouth Company "an absolute property
in all the American territory extending
from the fortieth to the forty-eighth degree of latitude and from the Atlantic to
the Pacific."   That large-handed grant
was qualified, to be sure, by the proviso
that colonies might not be planted in any
region "actually possessed or inhabited
by any other Christian prince or state";
but as England refused to acknowledge

that the Dutch had any possessions between the Virginia and the New England plantations, and as the English ambassador in Holland, Sir Dudley Carleton, lodged (February 9, 1622) a formal protest against the planting of the New Netherland colony, that proviso was no more than a politely turned phrase. On the other hand, the States General paid very little attention to the protest, and never formally replied to it. However, there it was on the record; and so was in readiness for use. But England went slowly in those days. Almost half a century passed before it was used. Mr. Chamberlain and Sir Alfred Milner were quicker in getting from cause to consequence a couple of years or so ago.

While the ambassadors talked — or maintained a discreet but aggravating silence—the merchants acted. In the years while the West India Company was in course of formation the foundation of the sea-wealth of New York was laid. The Dutch planted their trading-post on the island of Manhattan because the many water-ways which came together there obviously made it a good place for trade with the interior of the country. As exploration continued, the fact was demonstrated that it not only was a good place but that it absolutely was the best place for trade on the coast of North America: that there was no other such great land-locked harbor, which at once was near to the sea, easily open to it, and free from the dangers of outlying reefs and shoals; that nowhere else—and this fact continued to count first with us until the time of railroads—was there any such system of interior water-ways as that which made the Sandy Hook Chan-

54

nel the inlet to the trade of a vast part,
and a vastly rich part, of the continent.
Therefore the Dutch shallops went and
came on our thirteen rivers—and beyond
the shallop service, plying in the upper
reaches of those rivers and in countless
minor streams, was a still farther-reach-
ing service of canoes. And all of that
trade ebbed from and flowed to this island
of Manhattan: where the round-bellied
Dutch ships linked it with and made it a
part of the commerce of the world. Even
a minor prophet, with those geographical
facts in his possession, would not have
hesitated to prophesy a great future for
such a seaport with such a hold upon the
land.

When the West India Company came
into existence it therefore had among its
assets—although ignored in its chartered
list of assets—a little trading-post that

was in the way of promotion to be the
capital of a flourishing colony, had there
been manifested even a very small
amount of common sense and common
justice in the management of its affairs.
And at the beginning—being stimulated
to wise action, perhaps, by the English
assertion of a counter claim to their
American possessions—the Company did
go at the planting of New Netherland
with a certain show of energy, and on
lines of broader policy than were called
for by the mere requirements of trade.

Upon the completion of the Company's organization the management of
the affairs of New Netherland were con-
fided by the Directorate, the Council of
XIX., to the Chamber of Amsterdam—
whence came the name that was given to
the settlement on Manhattan Island—
and by that Chamber the first ship-load

of colonists, thirty families, was despatched from the Texel in the ship *New Netherland* in March 1623. Making their course
to the westward by a long reach into the
south—as was the habit of the Dutch
navigators, who ever were fearful of North
Atlantic storms—they touched at the
Canaries and at Guiana, and then beat
up the coast to Sandy Hook and made
their harbor early in May. (Possibly our
otherwise unaccounted-for custom of May-
day movings had its origin in their arrival
about May-day, and the consequent running of their yearly tenures from that
date.) They were of good stuff, those
colonists—mostly Walloons, very eager
to get away from European religious in-
tolerance for good and all. Their coming
marks the real founding of New York.
They were the first Europeans who came
to dwell upon this island with the inten-

tion of spending their lives here; and, in
the end—though that part of their intention was understood rather than stated—
of making themselves permanently a part
of it by being buried in its soil.

Meantime, by way of fortifying the
situation politically, the States General
erected into a Province the West India
Company's comet - like holding — which
had a tiny material head upon the sea-
board, and a vast vaporous tail that ex-
tended vaguely across the continent westward — and gave it, as a Province, the
heraldic rank and bearings of a Count.

Then it was that our beloved Beaver
came to us: the same worthy animal who
still figures gallantly in the arms of the
city of New York. As we first received
him, he was the single charge—" a beaver proper" — upon our shield, above
which a count's coronet was our crest.

58

Later, when new civic arms were granted to us by the English Crown—in the time of great commercial prosperity that followed upon the passage of the Bolting Act —he modestly joined the wind-mill sails and the flour - barrels, and so became a mere beaver "in chief and in base." And there he remains to this day: in lasting memorial of the fact that the foundation of the sea-wealth of this city was laid in its trade in furs.

3̣3

VII

AT the outset, the venture undertaken
by the West India Company was a
profitable one: not on the side of trade,
but on the side of war. Three great
successes marked the first ten years of
the Company's existence: the taking of
Bahia (1624), the capture of the treasure fleet (1628), and the reduction of
Pernambuco (1630). Of those three
events, although the Brazilian conquests
counted for more in the long run, the
capture of the plate-ships naturally made
the strongest impression upon the popular
mind. Indeed, that magnificent cash return upon invested patriotism is talked
about relishingly in Holland even until

this present day. And it is not surprising. Never has there been such a
bag of treasure in modern times! Admiral Peter Heyn, leaving out of the
account the vessels which he sunk with
their treasure in them, brought home to
Holland seventeen galleons laden with
bullion and merchandise valued, according to Dr. Asher, at more than fourteen—
or, according to the more conservative
Mr. Brodhead, at more than twelve mill-
ions of guilders; and the Dutch guilder
of that period, it must be remembered,
had a purchasing value not much less
than that of our dollar of to-day. Either estimate is prodigious—and on the
strength of those huge winnings the Company declared upon its paid-up capital a
dividend variously estimated by the same
authorities at fifty and at seventy-five
per cent. Neither the Standard Oil Com-

61

pany nor the Steel Trust as yet has
equalled that!

But it was not a wholesome sort of
money - making. "Successful war thus
poured infatuating wealth into the treasury of the West India Company," is the
view that Mr. Brodhead takes of it; and
he adds that when, in the ensuing year,
the King of Spain made overtures to renew the truce "the pride, the avarice,
and the religious sentiment of Holland
were united in continuing the war."
Against the truce the Company addressed
to the States General (November 16,
1629) a formal remonstrance. "We have
at present," declared the remonstrants,
"over one hundred full-rigged ships of
various burdens at sea . . . manned by
fifteen thousand seamen and soldiers and
armed with over four hundred metal
pieces . . . and over two thousand swiv-

els, beside pedereros to the number of
far beyond six hundred." That fleet had
not sailed the seas, nor was it intended
to sail the seas, for mere amusement—as
the remonstrants implied by adding that
" during some consecutive years " they
had " plundered the enemy and enriched
this country " by bringing into it great
stores of indigo, sugar, hides, cochineal
and tobacco; and, above all, by bringing
in the captured galleons—which contain-
ed " so great a treasure that never did any
fleet bring to this or to any other country
so great a prize." And they ended by
declaring that they had exhausted the
King of Spain's treasury by these various
appropriations of his property, and by
" depriving him of so much silver, which
was as blood from one of the arteries of
his heart." But the pith of their argument was in their assertion—in which

63

was more of truth than they suspected—
that "the utter ruin and dissolution of
this Company will be the result of the
present negotiations for a truce."

It was reasonable that the Company
should be so hot for keeping on with the
war. Spanish treasure-ships were to be
had for the mere taking—and the Dutch
found taking them very easy work indeed. It is a curious fact that the
Spaniards—who have done some very
pretty fighting at one time and another
on land—never were hard to whip at sea.
From the Armada down to Santiago their
naval record is a shabby one. We ham-
mered them pretty much as we pleased
in the nineteenth century; so did the
English in the eighteenth; so did the
Dutch in the seventeenth—the time that
I here am dealing with; and so, I believe
thoroughly, would the English have ham-

64

mered the whole Armada in the sixteenth had they not sublet a part of their contract to the winds and the waves.

The battlings of the Dutch and the Spaniards have a distinct place in our commercial annals, because one of their direct results was to check our commercial growth at the start. The "infatuating wealth" that poured in upon the West India Company tended to make it careless of the little colony of New Netherland, and also to make it resentful of the small return which that colony yielded upon the relatively large outlay required to keep it in running order: and so led to the adoption of the "squeezing" policy which handicapped the trade of the colonists and in the end destroyed their loyalty and made them welcome the change to English rule. Mr. Brodhead is within the mark in his observation:

"It was an evil day for New Netherland when the States General committed to the guardianship of a close and grasping mercenary corporation the ultimate fortunes of their embryo province in America."

In a report presented to the States General (October 23, 1629) the feeling of the Company in regard to its colony is made plain. "The people conveyed by us thither have . . . found but scanty means of livelihood up to the present time; and have not been any profit, but a drawback, to this Company. The trade carried on there in peltries is right advantageous; but, one year with another, we can at most bring home fifty thousand guilders."

Yet with that return, at that time, the Company should have been well satisfied. In *The Planter's Plea*, published in

66

EARLIEST KNOWN VIEW OF NEW AMSTERDAM. CIRCA 1630
Reversed (following Mr. I. H. Innes) from Joost Hartger's *Beschrijvingh van Virginia, Nieuw Nederlandt, etc.*

London in the year 1630, the English
author wrote that the colonists of New
Netherland "appeared to subsist in a
comfortable manner, and to promise fairly both to the State and to the undertakers." The trouble was that "the
undertakers" wanted too much and
wanted it too soon. In the year 1629
the population of the colony could not
have exceeded three hundred and fifty
souls; and three hundred and fifty people
very well might "subsist in comfort" on
an export trade of fifty thousand guilders a year. The Company in short, then
and always, was greedy. By holding New
Netherland as an investment rather than
as a trust, by laying heavy imposts upon
commerce in order to raise dividends, it
throttled the trade that a less selfish
policy would have left free to expand.

The one sort of private ownership in

the colony that was encouraged—by the
granting of little principalities to patroons, who were free within certain limitations to trade on their own account
—told directly against the welfare of the
mass of the colonists by creating unfair
distinctions of class. It was a trans-
planting of feudalism to America—and
feudalism did not thrive in American
soil. Actually, the patroonships were
bagged by an inside ring of the Company's directors—the practical value of
being on the ground floor was understood
in those days quite as well as we understand it now—and the outcome of that
intrinsically bad policy bred evil in two
ways. It created dissension in the management of the Company's affairs at
home by arraying inside private interests against the common interests of the
shareholders at large; and in the colony

the same private interests were arrayed against the common interests of the less-favored colonists. Later, the supply of arms which the savages obtained from the patroon trading - posts—but by no means only from those sources: trading guns for peltries was so profitable an illegal transaction that everybody was keen to have a hand in it—led on directly to the horrors of the Indian wars.

VIII

IN a word, atrociously bad government
was the rule almost from the beginning
until quite the end of the Dutch domination of New Netherland. Execrable administration in Holland led to execrable
executive management in the colony.
Excepting May (1624) and Verhulst
(1625), who were little more than factors,
the men sent out as governors (the official title was Director General) wretch-
edly neglected or absolutely betrayed the
interests which they were sworn to serve.

Kieft (1638–1646) was an easy first in
that bad lot. He was an ex-bankrupt,
whose bankruptcy had been of such sort
that his portrait had been hung up on the

town gallows. Against him, unrefuted, stood the pleasing charge of having embezzled ransom - money intrusted to him to rescue Christian captives held by the Turks. His evil work in New Netherland culminated in his provocation—by a horrid and utterly inexcusable massacre of savages — of the terrible Indian war of 1643: which brought the colony to the very verge of ruin, and which aroused so violent an outcry against him on the part of the colonists that he was recalled. In a way, justice was served out to him: he went down, his sins with him, in the wreck of the ship in which he took passage for home. But while Kieft holds the record for worse than incapacity, protests were made by the colonists against the doings of every one of the Directors—and always for cause. Each of them played first for his own

71

hand. After caring for himself, his care was for what remained of the interests of the Company—and those he either muddled or marred. Caring for the interests of the colonists, in every case, was the last consideration of all. Under those conditions, of necessity, discontent was chronic among the inhabitants of the Province from first to last.

On the other hand, I am persuaded that an archangel would have had his work cut out for him had he tried to govern at once wisely and acceptably the hustling, greedy, law-defying Dutchmen who dwelt in New Netherland two hundred and fifty years ago. By combining the atrocities of the Congo Free State under Lothair's administration (paralleled here by Kieft's atrocities) with the corruption at Johannesberg under Kruger's administration (paralleled here

72

by the corruption that obtained con-
tinuously under Dutch rule) we may get
a fair notion of what our few respectable
ancestors on this island had to contend
with, and of what our many unrespect-
able ancestors actually were.

The saving salt of those days was
found in the few men who stood resolutely for good government and for honest ways. They would have been called
mugwumps, had that word then been
available for use; and no doubt they did
receive some equivalent derogatory Dutch
name. The most exemplary of that
small but honorable company was David
Pietersz de Vries: who strove hard to
avert the Indian war waged by the outrageous Kieft, and who stood as distinctly for all that was good in the colony
as Kieft stood for all that was bad. Had
De Vries been appointed Director, in-

stead of Kieft, we should have been
saved from the blackest crime recorded
in our colonial history; and had he been
continued in office, in Stuyvesant's place,
the colony would not have fallen into
such disorder as to give the English a
mere walk - over when their time for
absorbing it came. No governor could
have prevented that absorption. It was
inevitable. But the community taken
over from De Vries would have been far
sounder morally than was that which
was taken over from Stuyvesant; and
therefore would have been less likely to
degenerate into a nest of pirates and
smugglers, as it did degenerate, during
the first thirty years of English rule.

Precisely what sort of government we
had here under the governors appointed
by the West India Company was set
forth with a refreshing candor in the

famous Remonstrance—and in its accom-
panying Memorial — presented by the
colonists to the States General in the
year 1649. Incidentally, the tone of
those documents—which are informed by
the petty spitefulness of mean spirits—
makes also an ugly case against their
authors; and the case is all the stronger
because it is to be read between the lines
of their complainings and is an alto-
gether unconscious arraignment of themselves. But this fact, while it tends to
palliate the minor charges against Stuyvesant—whose high - handed ways with
his subjects, and whose coarsely express-
ed contempt for them " in language better
befitting the fish-market than the Council board," probably were not without
justification—does not weaken the major charge of misgovernment preferred
against him and against the Company's

75

representatives generally; nor does it lessen the reasonableness of the several specific requests for reforms in law and in administration for which the remonstrants prayed.

The Remonstrance—a document that fills forty-four printed quarto pages—is a history of the planting of New Netherland, a description of the country, a statement of the wrongs suffered by the colonists, and a prayer for certain specified easements and reliefs. It was drawn up, presumably, by Adriaen van der Donck. It was signed by Van der Donck, Heermans, Hardenburg, Couwenhoven, Loockermans, Kip, Van Cortlandt, Jansen, Hall, Elbertsen, and Bout. Three of the signers, Van der Donck, Couwenhoven, and Bout, were delegated to take it to Holland and to lay it before the authorities at The Hague.

"In the infancy of this country" [wrote the complainants] "the Directors [the Board of Directors of the West India Company] adopted wrong plans, and in our opinion looked more to their own profit than to the country's welfare, and trusted more to interested than to sound advice. This is evident from the unnecessary expenses incurred from time to time; the heavy accounts from New Netherland; the taking of colonies [land grants] by Directors; their carrying on commerce, to which end trade has been regulated, and finally from not colonizing the country. . . . Had the Honble West India Company attended in the beginning to population instead of incurring great expense for things unnecessary . . . which through bad management and calculation came wholly to little or nothing, notwithstanding the excessive expenditure . . . the place might now be of considerable importance. . . .

"Trade, without which, when lawful, no country prospers, has also fallen off so much in consequence of the Company's acts that it is without a parallel, and more slavish than free, owing to high duties and all the inspections and trouble that accompany it. We highly approve of inspection according to the orders given by

77

the Company to its officers, and so far as 'tis
done to check smugglers, who have ruined the
country, and now go out from all parts; but it
ought, nevertheless, be executed without par-
tiality, which is not always the case. The
duty is high; of inspection and seizures there is
no lack, and thus lawful trade is turned aside
—except some little which is carried on only *pro
forma*, in order to push smuggling under this
cloak. Meanwhile the Christians are treated almost like Indians in the purchase of necessaries
which they cannot do without; this causes great
complaint, distress and poverty. Thus, for example: The merchants sell their dry goods, which
are subject to little loss, at a hundred per cent.
advance, and that freely, according as there is
a demand for, or a scarcity of, this or that
article; petty traders who bring small lots and
others who speculate, buy up those goods from
the merchants and sell them again to the common people who cannot do without them, often
at another advance of cent per cent., more or
less, according as they are persuaded or disposed. More is taken on liquors, which are
subject to a considerable leakage, and . . . the
goods are disposed by the first, second, and
third hands at an advance of one and two

hundred and more per cent. It would be impossible for us to enumerate all the practices
that are had recourse to for the purpose of
promoting self or individual interest; whilst
little thought is bestowed on introducing people
into the country. . . . It also has been seen
how the letters of the Eight Men have been
treated, and the result; besides many additional
orders and instructions which are not known
to us, and are alike ruinous. But laying this
aside for the present, with a word now and
again by way of remark, let us proceed to
examine how their [the Company's] servants,
and the Directors [of New Netherland] and
their friends, have fattened here from time to
time, having played with their employers and
the people as the cat plays with the mouse.
. . . We shall pass over the beginning . . . and
treat only of the two last sad and senseless ex-
travagances—we should say administrations—
of Director Kieft, which is now in truth past,
but its evil consequences remain; and of Director
Stuyvesant, which still stands—if that can be
said to stand which lies completely prostrate.
. . . Previous to Director Kieft's bringing the
unnecessary war upon the country, his principal
aim and object was to take good care of him-

self and to leave behind him a great name, but without any expense either to himself or to the Company. . . . With that view he considered the erection of a church very necessary. . . . The Director wished and insisted that it should be located in the Fort, where it was erected in spite of the others. And, truly, the location is as suitable as a fifth wheel to a coach; for, besides being small, the Fort lies on a point, which would be of more importance in case of population; the church, which ought to be owned by the people who defrayed the expense of its construction, intercepts and turns aside the Southeast wind from the gristmill which stands in that vicinity; and this is also one of the causes [!] why a scarcity of bread prevails frequently in summer for want of grinding. But this is not the sole cause; for the mill is neglected, and having been leaky most of the time, it has become decayed and somewhat rotten, so that it cannot now work with more than two arms, and has gone on thus for all of five years. But returning to the church, from which the gristmill has for the moment diverted us, the Director concluded, then, to have one built and on the spot which he preferred. He lacked money — and where was this to be got? It happened, about this time, that Everardus Bogardus, the clergyman, gave in marriage a daughter, by his first wife. The Director thought this a good time for his purpose, and set to work after the fourth or fifth drink; and he himself setting a liberal example, let the wedding guests sign whatever they were disposed to give towards the church. Each, then, with a light head, subscribed away at a handsome rate, one competing with the other; and although some heartily repented it when their senses came back, they were obliged, nevertheless, to pay—nothing could avail against it. The church, then, was located in the Fort, in opposition to every one's opinion. The honor and ownership of that work must be inferred from the inscription, which, in our opinion, is somewhat ambiguous, and reads thus: 'Anno 1642. Willem Kieft, Directeur Generael, heeft de gemeente desen temple doen bouwen.' But, laying that aside, the people nevertheless paid for the church."

That is the tone of the Remonstrance throughout. In a petty spirit it dealt with petty grievances at a length out of all proportion to their importance, and left what evidently were substantial grievances—as the high duties and the manifold inspections—far from clearly explained. That the complainants dismissed in a few lines the greatest of all the colonial crimes against good government and against humanity, Kieft's Indian war, was not surprising. The wreck of colonial interests which had been brought about by that war was well understood in Holland. There was no need that it should be explained.

IX

COLONIAL discontent usually is reasonable, and always is natural. It is reasonable, because colonies are pretty certain to be neglected, or remembered only to be harshly dealt with, by the home government. It is natural, because of the qualities pretty certainly inherent in colonists: who for the most part are either untried young men of strong character who know little of the world but are eager to make their way in it quickly, or incapable middle-aged men who have failed at home yet desperately hope to mend their broken fortunes abroad. Of the small residuum, the men who settle down to work and

83

who silently and steadfastly build their own fortunes by subduing a savage land, very little ever is heard. It is the "kickers" who make the noise. Here in America our sympathies always have been on the colonial side, and our animosities against home governments in general always have been strong. Perhaps, now that we are in the way of being (somewhat unwillingly) a "world power" ourselves, with swaggering and blustering colonies of our own, our point of view may change. It even is conceivable that in time we may come to have quite a compassionating fellow - feeling for our once tyrant, the late King George the Third!

Actually, in spite of bad laws badly administered, the colony of New Netherland did make headway. This country was a rich country, and its exploitation

VIEW OF NEW AMSTERDAM. CIRCA 1650. SHOWING THE CAPSKE ROCKS, NOW COVERED BY BATTERY PARK
(From the *Beschrijvingh van Amerika* of Arnoldus Montanus. Amsterdam, 1671)

—even under heavy handicaps—yielded a good return. In the year 1624 the cargo of furs sent home by Director May, "as a first year's remittance from New Netherland," sold for 28,000 guilders. Two years later the showing was still better. Under date of November 5, 1626, the following report was sent from Amsterdam to the States General:

"Yesterday arrived here the ship the *Arms of Amsterdam*, which sailed from New Netherland, out of the River Mauritius, on the 23d of September. They report that our people are in good heart and live in peace there. The women also have borne some children there. They have bought the Island Manhattes from the Indians for the value of 60 guilders—'tis 11,000 morgens [about 22,000 acres] in size. They had all their grain sowed by the middle of May, and reaped by the middle of August. They send thence samples of summer grain—such as wheat, rye, barley, oats, buckwheat, canary-seed, beans, and flax. The cargo of the aforesaid ship is: 7246 beaver skins, 178½ otter skins, 675 otter skins, 48 minck skins, 36 wild cat skins, 33 mincks, 34 rat skins. Considerable oak timber and hickory.''

Charles Wooley, writing half a century later, gives these values: "beaver skins, ordinary, 10 shillings; beaver skins, black, 15 shillings; minck skins, 5 shillings; otter skins, ordinary, 8 shillings; otter skins, black, if very good, 20 shillings." Roughly estimated, and without allowance for the fall in the value of peltries in that half century, the value of the cargo of the *Arms of Amsterdam* therefore was not less than $25,000—or well above $50,000, in the values of to-day. In another way the manifest of that ship is interesting. It is the earliest known manifest of a ship clearing from this port. The cargo seems to have been an exceptional one. In the year 1628 the exports hence "in two ships" is given at 61,000 guilders—only a trifle above the value of the lading of that single ship four years earlier—and for the years 1629–30 the exports were valued at 130,000 guilders. In the year 1632 the exports of furs alone were valued at 140,000 guilders, and in the year 1635 at 135,000 guilders. I must add, however, that the figures of that early time have a wandering way with them that places them anywhere but above reproach. Yet they show, at least, that returns of a respectable sort began almost immediately to come in from the colony, and that those returns increased from year to year.

With the development of trade between the colony and the home country went also the development of a trade that was wholly colonial. By the year 1635 a considerable commerce was carried on between New Netherland and

New England—of which the less important part was direct, and the more important part was the carriage of tobacco
and salt from Virginian and West Indian
ports to Boston. The suggestive fact also
is recorded that in the year 1637 a Dutch
ship sailing direct from the Texel landed
in Boston a cargo of sheep and oxen and
Flanders mares. Naturally, the English
did not take kindly to such commercial
under-cutting; and all the more naturally because the Dutch stiffly refused
to permit English traders to come upon
their own colonial preserves.

Touching those preserves, there was a
sharp little clashing of rights in April
1633, when the *William*, a London ship
commanded by a renegade Dutchman,
came into this port " to trade at Hudson's
river "—and peremptorily was refused a
trading license. There was a fine inter-

change of bravadoes between Director
Van Twiller and the *William's* captain.
Flags were run up and salutes were fired,
and there was a vast amount of vaporing
talk on the Director's side. But at the
end of it all the ship did go up the river
—being the first English vessel to ascend
the Hudson—and her captain would have
made his trade unmolested had not De
Vries put some stiffening into Van
Twiller's weak backbone. "If it had
been my case," said De Vries, shortly
and hotly, "I should have helped him
from the Fort to some eight-pound iron
beans!" "The English," he added, and
his remark has quite a modern ring in it,
"are of so haughty a nature that they
think everything belongs to them"; and
he concluded by declaring with energy:
"I should send the ship *Soutberg* after
him and drive him out of the river!" And

89

that was precisely what Van Twiller, being thus brought up to the collar, then did.

It was not in human nature, therefore, for the English quietly to permit Dutch ships to trade in English colonial ports when English ships were refused trading privileges in Dutch colonial ports; and, as a matter of fact, the profitable trade that was developed between New Netherland and the plantations in New England and Virginia—while immediately beneficial to the Dutch—was one of the most active of the several causes which led to the wresting from the Dutch of their holding in North America. The matter is too broad in its scope to be dealt with fully here; yet am I loath to relinquish it because of the many very human touches in which it abounds.

With one scrap of ancient history,

wherein the humanity still is fresh and
strong, I am justified in dealing: the famous case of the ship *Eendracht*—driven
by stress of weather into Plymouth in the
year 1632, and there seized by the English port authorities (I quote the Dutch
version of the matter) "on an untrue representation that the Peltries were bought
within the jurisdiction or district belonging to his majesty of Great Britain."
Over that seizure there was a diplomatic
squabble between Holland and England
that went on for years—and the whole of
it, I am persuaded, was the outcome of a
love-affair! According to a letter sent
by the States General to their Ambassador in England, the *Eendracht* was
"seized on false information of the
Provost of said ship . . . and of the
Pilot who, in opposition to the Director
and Skipper, being on shore got married."

There is the crux of it, I am sure. But
for that Pilot's impetuously inopportune
determination to wed the widow (I am
quite certain that she was a widow, because of the eagerness of it all) he very
probably could have taken the *Eendracht* out of Plymouth harbor and safe
away to sea. Being ordered, no doubt,
to do that very thing—and the widow
ashore waiting for him!—he and his
friend the Provost laid the "untrue representation" which led on to those years
of diplomatic blustering: but which also
led to the detention of the ship at Plymouth until he was safe wed to his bounc-
ing bride!

After all, what mattered it if Holland
and England were embroiled by that
brave Pilot's hot-hearted indiscretion?
Every man thinks first of his own happi-
ness; and in love-affairs—it has been so

from the world's beginning—he thinks of nothing else. I wish that we had the end of the story. Let us hope that his widow repaid him for his gallant defiance, for her sweet sake, of the orders of captains and directors, and that it turned out well—that sailor-wedding which shook two great states to their foundations nearly three centuries ago! In all seriousness, I am justified in recalling here that only half-told and long-forgotten idyl. It had its place, the love-making of that precipitate Pilot, among the causes which in time's fulness changed New Netherland and New Amsterdam into the State and City of New York.

X

UNDER spur of the "remonstrances"
—there were many of them—sent
home by the colonists, the States General
did make some effort to deal with New
Netherland on lines of equity. An official inquiry was made into the affairs
of the West India Company in the year
1638 that resulted in checking some of the
worst of the colonial abuses; and that
also led to the promulgation (1640) of a
new charter of Liberties and Exemptions
which materially added to the welfare of
the colony, and increased the comfort of
the colonists, by relaxing the regulations
under which trade was conducted and

by easing the conditions under which the people lived.

Kieft, be it said to his credit, gave effect to this liberal policy in so liberal a spirit that the three ensuing years—until almost ruin came with the Indian war —probably were the most prosperous in the time of Dutch rule. Notably, he encouraged English refugees, fleeing from religious persecution in New England, to settle in New Netherland; and those settlers—maintaining relations with their friends and kinsfolk — did much to develop the intercolonial trade of which I have written above. By the year 1642 the English were so numerous in New Amsterdam that the appointment of an official interpreter became necessary; and that officer also was required to serve as an intermediary between the Dutch merchants and the English ship-masters who broke the voyage between New England and the Virginia plantations by stopping here for a bit of trade.

It was for the accommodation of such wayfarers that the City Tavern—which later became the Stadt Huys—was built, facing Coenties Slip, in the year 1642; and it seems to have been built badly, as it manifested such a decided disposition to tumble to pieces in little more than half a century that it was torn down. I should be glad to believe that hospitality was the corner-stone of that nominally hospitable edifice; but I fancy that in building it some thought may have been taken of the fact that trade in a tavern is apt to turn in favor of the trader who has the hardest head— and it is an incontestable fact that our Dutch ancestors had heads upon which they could rely. Possibly some of those

96

THE TOWN HOUSE (STADT HUYS), NEW YORK, 1679
(Redrawn from the Dankers and Sluyter drawing. See *Memoirs of the Long Island Historical Society, vol. i.*)

visiting English skippers carried away in
their aching heads unkindly memories of
our City Tavern—as they beat down the
harbor and out through the Narrows on
their way to Virginia, or as they affront-
ed the dangers of Hell Gate on their way
eastward up the Sound!

The encouragement that Kieft gave to
the incoming of the English, and to the
trade with the neighboring English colonies, tended to the immediate good of New
Netherland; but in the end, of course, the
influx of those settlers, and the strain-
ing of relations with the government to
which they owed allegiance, were the
chief factors in hastening the downfall
here of Dutch rule. George Baxter, the
official interpreter — he seems to have
been a fuming sort of a person—was one
of the leaders of the rebellion that broke
out among the English on Long Island

in the year 1655; a rebellion that Stuyvesant's temporizing policy did not check,
and that helped to give a valuable part
of New Netherland to the English nine
years before they grabbed it all.

In another way Kieft's liberal administration of more liberal laws led on to
catastrophe. The increased freedom in
trading tended to facilitate the supply of
arms—in exchange for good bargains in
peltries—to the savages; and so enabled
the savages to make their winning fight
when, by Kieft's own abominable act, the
time for fighting came. From the very
beginning the trade in arms with the
Indians offered temptations too strong
to be resisted by the money - seeking
Dutch—just as it has offered temptations
too strong to be resisted by the money-
seekers of our own time on our western
frontier. Under Kieft it went on swim-

mingly. In those days a musket sold for twenty beaver skins, and a pound of gunpowder was worth in furs from ten to twelve guilders: and so the "bosch-lopers," or "runners in the woods," made their account with the savages—and gave no thought to the reaping of the whirlwind that was to come in sequence to that sowing of the wind.

Actually, the "bosch-lopers" were mere agents. The sources of supply of that pernicious trade were the capitalists of the colony. In the year 1644 a ship sent out from Holland by the Patroon of Rensselaerswyck — being searched by mere accident at New Amsterdam—was found to have on board, not on her manifest, "four thousand pounds of powder and seven hundred pieces, to trade with the natives." The illicit cargo was confiscated with a great show of propriety: but I do not doubt that the powder and the pieces got along to the natives in due course. In Stuyvesant's time (July 9, 1648) "Govert Barent, the armourer at Fort Amsterdam," and three others were arrested, and two of the four "were convicted and sentenced to death for violating the proclamation against the illicit trade in fire-arms." But the convicted and sentenced ones were not executed. "By the intervention of many good men" they got off from the hanging which they richly deserved, and nothing worse happened to them than the confiscation of their illegally held property. In other words, public sentiment was in favor of the trade—in which, practically, everybody desired to have a hand—and no real attempt was made to suppress it because the rulers of the colony shared the popular feeling and either were weak or were venal, and for the most part were both. The responsibility for that sin, as for many others, therefore rests primarily with the West India Company: which without exception, from Van Twiller's time onward, appointed as Directors of New Netherland men utterly unfitted to perform the gravely important duties with which they were charged.

As was shown by the official inquiries made from time to time into the affairs of the colony, usually followed by small reforms, the Dutch government was not wholly unmindful of the evils wrought by the mercenary corporation to which it had delegated too great powers; but, the initial error of delegating those powers having been committed, not even the States General could set right what had begun by being, and what continued until the end to be, hopelessly wrong. From the start, that ill-conceived colonial venture had in it the seeds of failure. The wonder is not that it ended so soon, but that it lasted so long.

XI

WHEN Peter Stuyvesant, the last of those incompetent Directors, took over the government of New Netherland (May 11, 1647) things were in a hopelessly bad way. Mr. Brodhead, whose disposition is to make the best of Dutch shortcomings, thus summarizes the situation: "Excepting the Long Island settlements, scarcely fifty bouweries could be counted; and the whole province could not furnish, at the utmost, more than three hundred men capable of bearing arms. The savages still were brooding over the loss of sixteen hundred of their people. Disorder and discontent prevailed among the commonalty; the public

revenue was in arrear, and smuggling had
almost ruined legitimate trade; conflicting claims of jurisdiction were to be
settled with the colonial patroons; and
jealous neighbors all around threatened
the actual dismemberment of the province. Protests had been of no avail; and
the decimated population, which had
hardly been able to protect itself against
the irritated savages, could offer but a fee-
ble resistance to the progress of European
encroachment. Under such embarrassing
circumstances the last Director General
of New Netherland began his eventful
government." And to this Mr. Brodhead
might have added in set terms what he
does add virtually by his subsequent presentment of facts: that Peter Stuyvesant,
so far from being the man to set a wrong-
going colony right, was precisely the man
to set a right-going colony wrong.

Irving, with his accustomed genial warping of the truth, has created so kindly a caricature of the last of the Dutch governors that our disposition is to link him with, almost to exalt him to the level of, the blessed Saint Nicholas —our city's Patron. Such association is not justified by the facts, and our good Saint—notwithstanding his notable charity and humility—most reasonably might take exception to it. In truth, Stuyvesant had little in common with any respectable saint in the calendar; and to come upon the real man—as he is revealed in the official records of his time —is to experience the shock of painful discovery.

The Remonstrance of the year 1649, already cited, while dealing generally with the manifold misfortunes brought upon the colonists by bad government, deals particularly with the misdoings of the last Director: who then had been in office for only two years and a half, and who in that time had succeeded in setting the whole colony by the ears. "His first arrival," declared the remonstrants, "was peacock-like, with great state and pomposity"; and the burden of their complaint, constantly recurred to, is of his brutally dictatorial methods and of his coarsely arrogant pride. "His manner in court," they declare, "has been ... to browbeat, dispute with, and harass one of the two parties; not as beseemeth a judge, but like a zealous advocate. This has caused great discontent everywhere, and has gone so far and had such an effect on some that many dare not bring any suits before the court if they do not stand well, or passably so, with the Director; for whom he opposeth hath both sun and moon against him. . . . He likewise frequently submits his opinion in writing . . . and then his word is: 'Gentlemen, this is my opinion, if any one have ought to object to it, let him express it.' If any one then, on the instant, offer objection . . . his Honour bursts forth, incontinently, into a rage and makes such a to do that it is dreadful; yea, he frequently abuses the Councillors as this and as that, in foul language better befitting the fish-market than the Council board; and if all this be tolerated, he will not be satisfied until he have his way." In regard to the right of appeal to the home government, his declaration is cited that "People may think of appealing during my time — should any one do so, I would have him made a foot shorter, pack the pieces off to Holland, and let him appeal in that way." And to this the remonstrants added by way of comment: "Oh cruel words! What more could a sovereign do?"

As the tone of the complainings shows, there was another side to all this. According to his lights (which were few) and within his limitations (which were many) Stuyvesant was in the way of being a reformer: and reformers ever have been painted blackest by those whom they sought to reform. That outrageous little colony needed a deal of reforming when he took over its government; and had his mandatory proclamations stopped with the one that forbade "sabbath breaking, brawling, and drunkenness," he still would have had a hornets' nest about his ears. Fancy what would have been the consensus of opinion on the part of the leading citizens of Fort Leavenworth

had any reforming person fired off at
them a proclamation of that sort in the
old days of the Santa Fé Trail! But
Stuyvesant's reforms cut deeper. Not
content with trying to reduce to decency
the energetic social customs of the colonists, he tried also to bring them up to the
line of honest dealing: and so struck at
their pockets as well as at their hearts.
He forbade the sale of liquor to the
savages: a most profitable business in
itself, and of much indirect advantage
to those engaged in it — because an in-
toxicated savage obviously was more
desirable than a sober savage to bargain
with for furs. He made stringent regulations which checked the profitable
industry of smuggling peltries into New
England, and European goods thence
into New Netherland. He issued revo-
lutionary commands that the frowsy

109

and draggle-tailed little town should be
set in order and cleansed. And on top
of all this, farther to replenish the exhausted treasury of the colony, he levied
a tax upon liquors and wines. That was
the climax of his offending. As the out-
raged and indignant colonists themselves
declared—becomingly falling back upon
holy writ for a strong enough simile—
the wine and liquor tax was "like the
crowning of Rehoboam!"

It is not surprising that such a community should be at odds with such a
ruler. Nearly half a century later, when
New Amsterdam had become New York,
a like resentful commotion was stirred
up by another and a far better reform
governor, Lord Bellomont: who was sent
out from England to put down, and
who did put down, the pirates and smugglers then flourishing in this town. But

Lord Bellomont was a strong man and a just man—who carried through his reforms to a masterly finish precisely because his sense of justice restrained him from making an arbitrary use of his strength. Stuyvesant was neither strong nor just, and he was arbitrary to the last degree. Considering the material that he had to work on, and considering also the manners and customs of his times, his headstrong ways and his coarse speech admit of palliation. No doubt he gave those equally headstrong and equally foul-mouthed colonists pretty much what, in one way, they deserved. But provocation is not justification. The capital error of his government was not its harshness but its arbitrary harshness. He seems to have been a waspish little man, with a testy temper that ever disposed him to fly into a rage with any-

body who in the smallest particular con-
tradicted him; and, assuredly, he lacked
the sagacity that might have saved him
from letting fly his choleric outbursts with
an indiscriminating violence that destroyed the moral effect of what very often, no
doubt, was his righteous wrath.

Under such a government as Stuyvesant gave to that unfortunate colony
there could be no real improvement in its
affairs. Even when his attempted reforms were sound—and for the most part
they were sound—the effect of them was
weakened, and their realization was made
difficult or impossible, by the manner in
which they were applied.

THE VISSCHER MAP, WITH A VIEW OF

XII

B^{UT} a better man than Stuyvesant
—while he might have lost it with
more dignity—could not have saved to
Holland the colony of New Netherland.
Forces from within and forces from without were working for its destruction. In-
ternally, its affairs were administered with
incompetence tempered with injustice—
and it owed its bad government to the
fact that it was but a by-venture in a
great scheme of combined money-making
and statecraft; and to the farther fact
that it was more and more neglected,
or remembered only to be more tightly
squeezed, as the ruinous end of the West
India Company drew near.   Externally,

the English constantly were pressing more closely upon its borders: strong in their determination to have the whole of it; and in the mean time taking possession of such scraps of it—as the eastern end of Long Island—as dropped loose of their own accord. Such conditions led inevitably to the loss of that which never had been well held.

The evil star of the West India Company was the most conspicuous among the several stars in their courses which fought against the Dutch in their struggle to hold fast to their American colonies. The condition of the Company never was sound financially. By heroic marauding it did acquire a vast sum of money—which went as quickly as it came. But the Company absolutely failed to build up in any part of its dominions a substantial legitimate trade from which it

could draw securely a stable revenue. Its
nearest approach to founding a well-
ordered colony was in the Brazils, under
the one competent governor that it ever
sent out from Holland: Count John
Maurice of Nassau. Under the wise rule
of that excellent ruler a liberal scheme
of trade regulations was established; religious toleration was assured; and for all
classes alike there was just enforcement
of, and equal protection under, a just code
of laws. But, to quote Dr. Asher, "even
Count John Maurice's brilliant talents
yielded no pecuniary profits. Compelled
by the strict and reiterated orders of the
Directors of the Company, he had to carry
on an incessant war with the Portuguese
in southern Brazil. Great part of his revenue consisted of booty; and his troops
ruined more than they took away—drawing upon the Dutch possessions similar

115

acts of retribution from the enraged
enemy. Among those horrors of border
warfare agriculture and trade could not
survive." If such a state of affairs obtained in the best managed of the Company's colonies, and at a time when the
Company was in a flourishing condition,
we need not be surprised that the state
of affairs in its worst managed colony—
our own New Netherland — became almost unendurable as the Company drew
nearer and nearer to collapse.

From the year 1630 onward the Company's finances showed, as Dr. Asher puts
it, "a terribly constant downward ten-
dency." Only a year after it had paid its
famous dividend upon its treasure-ship
winnings, and out of its remaining sur-
plus had lent 600,000 guilders to the
Dutch government, it was unable to meet
its running expenses. Under its charter

it was entitled to a subsidy; but the
government—partly because of lack of
funds, but more because of the adverse
action taken by the dominant political
ring—was slack in making the promised
payments and the subsidy fell badly into
arrear. Money from other sources was
not forthcoming. No colonial trade of
importance had been developed; and the
plan for breaking Spain's line of communication with her colonial treasure-
houses had been executed so effectively
that it had reacted upon its projectors
after the manner of a boomerang; that
is to say, although the Company had to
carry the load of an armed fleet created
mainly to bag Spanish plate-ships, the
seas were empty of plate-ships to be
bagged.

Bad luck had something to do with
the Company's misfortunes, but at the

117

root of them was bad management. The same stupidity, or worse, that was shown in the conduct of the affairs of our own little New Netherland was shown on a larger scale in the conduct of the far more important affairs in Brazil. At the end of a long series of quarrels with the Council, Count John Maurice resigned his commission in disgust in the year 1644. His successors, for the most part, were incompetents. When they happened to possess wits they used them in betraying the Company's interests—for a consideration—to the Portuguese. It took just ten years of that sort of thing to bring matters to their logical climax. In the year 1654 the Company's troops evacuated the Brazils.

Ten years more brought the end of everything. Dr. Asher puts the record of those ten calamitous years into a few words. "We cannot here attempt," he writes, "to describe the Company's last agony: its vain attempts to combine with the East India Company; its painful efforts to obtain from the government either armed assistance or payment of its arrears. The symptoms of bankruptcy became saddening and more threatening from year to year. At last its creditors began to seize the Company's property. The death blow was struck in 1664— when New Netherland, the Company's last valuable possession, was conquered by the English." And so that rather grandly conceived, but consistently ill executed enterprise, came to a miserable end. As a warning, the history of its few triumphs and of its many failures has a permanent value. And especially does its history point the moral that it is unwise, to say the least, to try to get from invested patriotism a dividend in cash.

Conceivably, by the exercise of a small amount of common sense, the Dutch might have retained their holdings in Brazil; but from their holdings in North America — New Netherland, and the colony on the Delaware—the common sense of all the ages could not have saved them from being squeezed out. There they were at grips with a race stronger than their own in numbers, and not less strong in sheer grit. For thirty years before the end came, the English were pressing in upon their territory from the east and from the south; while across seas, with a large statesmanship, the English government was taking a hand in putting on the screws.

The most effective twist of the English screw was the passage by the Common-

wealth Parliament (October 9, 1651) of
the Navigation Act: which decreed that
goods imported into England must come
in English ships or in ships belonging to
the country in which the goods were
produced. As the Dutch at that time
had the carrying trade of the world pretty
well in their hands, the English law was
in the nature of some of our own highly
impersonal legislation affecting "cities of
the first class." No names were mention-
ed—but it hit where it was meant to hit,
and it hit hard. A loud buzzing of ambassadors followed that shot at Dutch
commerce. But the propositions made
by Holland—that there should be free
trade to the West Indies and to Virginia,
and that "a just, certain, and immovable
boundary line" should be fixed between
the English and the Dutch territories in
America—came to nothing; and so, pres-

121

ently, there was the louder buzzing of guns. In the handsome little war that followed (1652–54), the English — while practically gaining what they fought for —experienced the unusual sensation of being soundly whipped at sea. Blake fairly was driven to take shelter in the Thames: after which Tromp went sailing up and down the Channel with that aggravating broom at his mast - head, to which reference is inexpedient in talking with the average Englishman even now.

Here in Manhattan there was a great show of bellicosity while that waspish little war went on. It was then—under orders from Holland to put the town in a state of defence—that our famous wall was built along the line of what now is Wall Street. Thomas Baxter (who proved himself to be a very bad lot, a little later) had the contract for supplying the pali-

122

sadoes which were intended to stand off his own countrymen; but which, in point of fact, never stood off anything more dangerously aggressive than wandering cows. Also, the city watch was strengthened; and preparations for a naval demonstration (in the event of a hostile fleet appearing before the city) were made by ordering Schipper Visscher "to keep his sails always ready, and to have his gun loaded day and night." In a word, we all were full of fight in that strenuous time—but, mercifully, carnage was averted. It takes two armies to make a battle: and the English army, for which we were waiting in so blood-thirsty a mood, discreetly remained at a safe distance from our pugnacious little fume of a town.

XIII

STUYVESANT showed both manliness and good common sense in dealing with the most threatening feature of that really volcanic situation: the charge made by the New-Englanders that he had endeavored to stir up against them an Indian revolt. He met the charge promptly by inviting the Commissioners* to send delegates to New Amsterdam to investigate it—and when they came he refuted it. More than that, he submitted

* The colonies of New Plymouth, Massachusetts, Connecticut and New Haven became confederated, May 19, 1643, as "The United Colonies of New England." The administration of the affairs of the confederacy was intrusted to a board consisting of two commissioners from each colony.

to the delegates very reasonable and just propositions for the regulation of inter-colonial affairs. In substance, those propositions were: I. Neighborly friendship, without regard to the hostilities in Europe; II. Continuance of trade as before; III. Mutual justice against fraudulent debtors; IV. A defensive and offensive alliance against common enemies. But the delegates refused to entertain his propositions, and went back to Boston in an unexplained but quite unmistakable huff. Very likely they had an instinctive feeling that treaties were unnecessary—since, without treaties, things were coming their way.

Moreover, the desire of the New-Englanders to fight the Dutch was strong. Patriotism may have been at the root of that desire, but its more obvious motive was a mere commonplace human longing

to lay hands on valuable Dutch property.
Rhode Island—in those years, and for
many succeeding years, the abode of
notoriously hard characters—even made
a start at a little war of spoliation on its
own account. Two loose fish of thievish
proclivities, Dyer and Underhill, were
granted a license by that disreputable
colony (June 3, 1653) to "take all Dutch
ships and vessels as shall come into their
power"; and the energetic Thomas Baxter—fresh from his palisading operation
in Wall Street, and very likely using the
profits of that operation in fitting out his
expedition—also got a predatory license
from Rhode Island ("turned pirate," is
the way that Mr. Brodhead puts it) and
made a spirited looting cruise along the
Sound: that was ended by his being "run
in" not by the Dutch but by the authorities of New Haven.

Only the action of Massachusetts at that juncture averted what would have been a most horrid little war between the Dutch and the English colonies; and, as it was, the war was escaped by a very close shave. The delegates, being come again to Boston, presented their report of the evidence that had been laid before them, in New Amsterdam and elsewhere, for and against the alleged Dutch plot to excite an Indian rising; and the matter was referred to a conference of "divers neighbouring elders," held before the General Court of Massachusetts, with instructions to find out "what the Lord calleth to do." The elders found proofs enough to "induce them to believe" in the reality of "that late execrable plot, tending to the destruction of so many dear saints of God, which is imputed to the Dutch governor and fiscal"; but they

127

did not find the proofs "so fully conclu-
sive as to clear up present proceedings
to war." Thereupon the General Court
voted that they were not "called to make
a present war with the Dutch."

That mild decision was not well received. Voicing the popular feeling —
and with the bellicose tendencies of his
cloth — the "teacher of the church at
Salem" wrote to urge immediate hostilities: the postponement of which, he
declared, already "had caused many a
pensive heart." Six out of the eight
Commissioners were at one with this
kindly gentleman in his desire for vica-
rious blood - letting. Solidly they cast
their votes for instant war. Fortunately,
the members of the General Court of
Massachusetts kept their heads. Rest-
ing their opinion upon the terms of the
colonial Articles of Confederation, they

declared that it was beyond the powers
of "six commissioners of the other colonies to put forth any act of power in a
vindictive war, whereby they shall command the colonies dissenting to assist
them in the same." That declaration—
which virtually was a declaration, nearly two centuries in advance of its recog-
nized existence, of the doctrine of State
Rights—saved the day. The Commissioners sent to Stuyvesant "a peevish reply":
telling him that his "confident denials
of the barbarous plot charged will weigh
little in the balance against such evidence" as that which they had secured;
and adding the broad and vague threat
that "we must still require and seek due
satisfaction and security." But their
vapering led to nothing, and the war
did not come off. Massachusetts spoke
the final word—in reply to a request

9   129

from Connecticut that "by war, if no other means will serve, the Dutch at and about the Manhatoes, who have been and still are like to prove injurious and dangerous neighbours, may be removed." To that intemperate request the temperate answer was given that Massachusetts refused to act "in so weighty a concernment as to send forth men to shed blood" unless satisfied "that God calls for it; and then it must be clear and not doubtful, necessary and expedient."

That persistent stand for peace was due in part, no doubt, to the fact that between Massachusetts and New Netherland there was no such sharp conflict of interests as there was between New Netherland and the nearer-lying English colonies; that, on the contrary, there was even a certain friendliness between the two because of the trade that went on, to

their common advantage, between Boston and New Amsterdam. But I think
that what really prevented the war was
Stuyvesant's promptness and frankness
in dealing with the charge that he had
sought to stir up an Indian revolt. The
clearness of his defence, and his straight-
forward way of making it, constituted an
appeal to the sense of right which then
and always was characteristic of the
Massachusetts colonists; and that appeal,
I am persuaded, counted for more with
them than did the feeling of friendliness
begotten of common interests in trade.

The fact is to be noted that Stuyvesant
uniformly showed in what may be termed
his foreign policy a far greater wisdom
than he usually showed in his domestic
policy. His one important aggressive act
—his reduction (1655) of the Swedish
colony on the Delaware, in dealing with

131

which Irving has quite outdone himself in a farrago of mingled nonsense and falsehood—was admirably planned and most successfully executed. He gained his end, without any fighting whatever, by the menacing display of an effective superior force: a method, it will be observed, that accords precisely with the rules laid down by the highest modern authorities on the art of war. It is true that in the Treaty of Hartford (1650) he yielded too much to the English; but his concessions materially lessened the dangerous border troubles, and the treaty certainly was beneficial for a time. His dealings with Virginia were to still better purpose. Even while the war between Holland and England was in progress—in accordance with his desire, scouted by the New-Englanders, for "neighbourly friendship, without regard to the hostil-

132

ities in Europe"—he made two attempts to conclude a commercial treaty with the Virginia authorities; and he succeeded in effecting with them a favorable working arrangement in the year 1653 that led on to the more formal and equally favorable convention of the year 1660.

The Virginia trade began to be of importance in the year 1652, when the export tax on tobacco shipped from New Netherland was removed; a concession on the part of the Amsterdam Chamber with which were united a reduction of the price of passage from Holland outward, and permission—here was the beginning of our slave trade—for the colonists to import negroes from Africa. A hint of trade direct with the Spanish colonies is found, also, in a list of charges brought (1653) by the West India Company against the proprietors of Rensselaer-

wyck; one of those charges being that
"licenses have been granted to private individuals to sail to the coast of Florida."

I should like to follow up that interesting lead, but there is little to go upon in
the indiscreetly reticent records of the
time. One other important trace of it
I have found: in a letter (February 13,
1659) from the Amsterdam Chamber to
the Director General and Council in New
Netherland granting "a larger liberty to
the inhabitants there to trade . . . to
France, Spain, Italy, the Caribbee islands,
and other parts, to dispose of and sell
their freighted products, salted fish, wares
and merchandise"; subject to the restric-
tion that they "shall be obliged and
bound to return direct either here before
this city of Amsterdam or back to New
Netherland to the place of your Honours'
abode, in order to pay to your Honours,

on the discharge and sale thereof, such duties as the Company here derives from them." Bearing on this matter, but a little beside it, is a minute (July 10, 1655) of the States General touching a memorial presented by the Spanish ambassador requesting that one "Sebastien Raef, a Captain or privateer committing piracies in the West Indies on the subjects of the Most Illustrious King" should be arrested in Amsterdam; and "that the government of New Netherland be instructed to arrest in their harbours Joan van Kampen, his lieutenant, together with his ship and effects, that law and justice be administered to the one and the other, for the behoof of the interested, with infliction of exemplary punishment for the piracies they have committed." From which we may infer that somewhat liberal notions obtained in New Netherland as to the scope of commercial relations with the colonies of Spain.

Putting incidental piracies out of the question, Stuyvesant certainly endeavored—according to his lights—to foster the foreign trade of New Netherland. His voyage to the West Indies in the year 1655 was made expressly to that end; and his consistent effort seems to have been to make New Amsterdam a little metropolis in which should centre the American colonial trade. Possibly I am going too far in crediting him with the deliberate formulation and pursuit of a policy in which was such large statesmanship; but it is, at least, an interesting and a suggestive fact that most of his plans touching the exterior affairs of the colony do wear the look of having been conceived in the spirit of one who had that great end in view.

136

Unfortunately, Stuyvesant did not show in dealing with home matters the excellent qualities which he showed in dealing with intercolonial matters. Had he done so his record would have been a very different one, and his governorship —while ending in the always inevitable loss of his province—would have ended without disgrace. The shame of the taking of New Netherland by the English was not that it was conquered; it was that its people—in their eagerness to escape from a government that had become intolerable — almost welcomed their conquerors. But only the more because of his bad domestic policy does the last Director need the praise, that assuredly is due to him, for his good foreign policy; and most of all does he deserve praise for his share—a good half of the credit belongs to Massachusetts—in so handling the matters at issue with the New England colonies as to avert a war in which the meanest sordid motives would have found vent in a truly horrible way. I suppose that there can be nothing more despairingly cruel than a fight to the death, having greed for its motive, between two castaways on a desert island in a lonely sea: and it would have been much that sort of a fight between the handful of English and the handful of Dutch, then living remote and isolated in the American wilderness, had they come to blows.

THE ALLAERDT VIEW OF NEW YORK. CIRCA 1668
(From the map of Reinier and Josua Ottens)

XIV

IN the thick of that troublous time, while Holland and England were at open war and while the threat of war hung over their dependent colonies, the long-cherished desire of New Amsterdam to become a city was realized. As a matter of course, it was not realized in a satisfactory way—nothing was satisfactory to anybody, to state the case broadly, in which the West India Company had a hand; but, at least, on February 2, 1653, the civic government was established which, in one form or another, has been maintained on this island until this present day.

By the terms of the grant, from the

Amsterdam Chamber, the municipal organization of New Amsterdam was to resemble "as much as possible" that of the parent city in Holland; but, as the matter worked out in practice, the possibilities proved to be so limited that the resemblance was in the nature of a caricature. Stuyvesant set up and maintained his right to appoint the members of the city government — the burgomasters, schepens, secretary, and schout —with the natural result that his authority continued to be paramount in civic matters; and in general he contrived to make the new order of things very much the same as the old order so far as any real increase of liberties was concerned. In a word, as Mr. Brodhead puts it: "The ungraceful concessions of the grudging Chamber were hampered by the most illiberal interpretation which their provincial representative could devise." For Mr. Brodhead — whose disposition toward the Director uniformly is kindly — those are very strong words. But they are amply justified by the facts.

With a modernity of method that our citizens of that period resented more keenly (being unaccustomed to it) than we resent it now, Stuyvesant made out his "slate"; and then—with a directness that a Tammany leader would weep over in envy—put in his men by the simple process of issuing a proclamation in which they were assigned to their several offices. Save in our spasmodic lucid intervals of civic reform, we still get by ways only a trifle more roundabout to just the same practical results—and philologists, with these early facts available for their study, will perceive with pleasure the nice linguistic propriety that there is in our

141

present use of the Dutch word "boss."
On the very instant that this city became a city the political meaning of
that word, in effect, was established and
defined.

Some of the men named on Stuyvesant's "slate," as is the custom nowadays, were respectable citizens. More of
them, still in accordance with modern
custom, were not. And — fitting to a
hair with Tammany methods—the most
important office was given to the worst
of them all. For Schout—an official who,
in addition to presiding over the Board of
Burgomasters and Schepens, performed
duties which in a way combined those
of our modern sheriff and district attor-
ney—Stuyvesant appointed Cornelis van
Tienhoven, the Company's Fiscal: and
had he searched through the whole colony he probably could not have found a

142

man more outrageously unfit for any
office at all.

In the summary, prepared by order of
the States General, of the Remonstrance
of 1649, Van Tienhoven is thus pleasingly
described: "He is subtle, crafty, intel-
ligent, sharp witted for evil; one of the
oldest inhabitants in the country; is con-
versant with all the circumstances both
of Christians and Indians, hath even
associated with the savages through
lechery; he is a dissembler, double-faced,
a cheat; the whole country proclaims
him a knave, a murderer, a traitor, in-
asmuch as he by false reports originated
the war [the Indian war of 1643]. He
holds the office of Secretary, wherein he
perpetrates all conceivable sorts of blun-
ders, now against one, now against another, even against his own employers;
he fleeces the people."

To this arraignment may be added the testimony of Hendrick van Dyck, given a year earlier (1652) when he was superseded in his office of Fiscal by—to use his own kindly words—"the perjured, godless Cornelis Tienhoven." Van Dyck uplifted his testimony in these terms: "Were an honorable gentleman put in my place, the false accusations which the Director [Stuyvesant] made and sent over against me long ago might have some semblance of truth; but his perjured secretary, Cornelis van Tienhoven, who returned hither contrary to the prohibition of their High Mightinesses; who is known, and can be proved to all the world, to be a * * * and perjurer; who is a disgrace to, and the sole affliction of, Christians and heathens in this country, and whom the Director always hath managed to shield—this is the person whom

144

the Director hath of his own authority appointed Fiscal!" It is only just to add that Van Dyck's genial deliverance was made against a man who had ousted him from a lucrative office and also, as is apparent, while he himself was under fire. Obviously, he had his little prejudices, and he certainly did not hesitate to express them with an engaging frankness. But the fact remains that everything in his statement is borne out by the records—excepting, perhaps, the assertion that Van Tienhoven was "the sole affliction of Christians and heathens." That is too exclusive. The Christians and heathens resident in New Amsterdam were variously and very generally afflicted in those unhappy days.

Touching the affair of Van Tienhoven and poor Lysbet van Hoogvelt, "the daughter of the basket-maker in Amsterdam," the dry and formal records of two centuries and a half ago suddenly cease to be dry and formal and become warmly alive. It is inexpedient to quote in full the several long depositions taken in Holland in the matter, and it also is needless: a few extracts from those ancient documents will suffice to make the case clear. Louisa Noë, "who speaks by her woman's troth, instead of oath," testified that there came to her "to engage lodgings for himself and a young lady . . . a certain corpulent and thickset person, of red and bloated visage and light hair, who she afterward understood was called Van Tienhoven." Margaretta van Eeda, "tavern - keeper in old Haerlem at the Sluice," bearing witness "upon her veracity and conscience, instead of upon oath," testified—in more kindly terms as to my gentleman's personal appear-

ance—that "over a year ago there came
to lodge at her house a likely person of
ruddy face, corpulent body, and having
a little wen on the side of his cheek, who
she afterward understood was from New
Netherland, having with him a woman
toward whom he evinced great friendship
and love, calling her always 'Dearest,'
and conversing with her as man and wife
are wont to do." Elizabeth Janns, inn-
keeper, of The Arms of Haerlem, testified
that "a person named Mr. Cornelis van
Tienhoven came divers times to the
house of the deponent, keeping open
tavern . . . with Lysbet Janssen Croon
van Hoogvelt . . . and have there at
different times, now and then, eaten fish
and showed and manifested toward each
other great love and friendship, such as
is the custom among sweethearts." And
the end of the story is told in a letter

written here in Manhattan by Augustin
Heermans, September 20, 1651: "The
basket - maker's daughter, whom Van
Tienhoven brought from Holland on a
promise of marriage, coming here and
finding he was already married, hath
exposed his conduct even in the public
court." That exposure, as is evident,
did him no harm. Less than a year
later Stuyvesant appointed him Fiscal,
and less than two years later appointed
him Schout—and so made him the chief
officer of the then new-born city that
now is New York.

I have dwelt at length upon Van
Tienhoven's personal record, and I have
revived this ancient scandal in which
poor Lysbet had so cruel a part (and, too,
after they had "eaten fish and showed
and manifested toward each other great
love and friendship"!) because such de-

tailed statement is necessary to support convincingly my general assertions touching the immorals of the inhabitants and of the rulers of this unfortunate town. There was, indeed, a popular outcry against Van Tienhoven's appointment; but it seems to have been based mainly on the ground that he was unfit to be Schout because he still continued to be an officer, the Fiscal, of the Company—not on the broader and very tenable ground that he was an unfit person to hold any public office at all. And, also, the outcry came in part—as in the case of the shady Van Dyck, who had been "turned down" in Van Tienhoven's favor—from citizens whose right to object to anybody on the score of immorals was of a highly attenuated sort. In the end, to be sure, he was turned out of his office in disgrace by order of the West India Company; and

149

Stuyvesant was forbidden again to employ him — or to employ his brother, Adriaen, who had been detected in fraud as receiver general—in the public service. But that order was a lashing of Stuyvesant over Van Tienhoven's shoulders, and it was not issued until Van Tienhoven had been Schout of the city for three years. Even Tammany has not beaten this record in civic immorality which our city scored at its very start.

XV

ON December 10, 1653, "the most important popular convention that had ever been assembled in New Netherland," to quote Mr. Brodhead's words, met in the Stadt Huys of New Amsterdam. That convention — being a gathering of representatives of the capital city, of the near-by Dutch towns, and of the English towns on Long Island—was in the way of being an impotent parliament: that came together not as a governing and law - making body but to remonstrate against the existing government, and against the tangle of inequitable laws (still farther complicated by arbitrary edicts) in which the colonists were involved.

What gave that queer little parliament its chief significance was the presence, for the first time in Dutch councils, of English delegates; and the fact that those delegates came to the council rightfully, as representatives of their fellow - countrymen legally subject to the government of New Netherland, did not make them any the less representatives of the race that was crowding out the Dutch from their holding in the new world.

It was at the instance of the English, indeed, that the council was convened. Long Island had been filling up steadily with English settlers, and those settlers took even less kindly than did the Dutch to the eccentricities and the inefficiencies of the government under which they lived. Especially did they resent the failure of that government to protect them against the many little freebooters

—of the Thomas Baxter stripe—who committed highly annoying robberies along the borders of the Sound; and against the many stray savages who, as occasion offered, engaged in little ravagings and murderings of a distasteful sort. Also, they had the characteristic English longing to be let alone in the management of their local affairs. Out of which conditions arose among them the not unreasonable desire either to be taken care of, or to be given a free hand in taking care of themselves.

In order to talk matters over with the Dutch authorities, representatives came up from Gravesend and Flushing and Newtown; and a conference was held in the Stadt Huys (November 26, 1653) to consider what could be done "for the welfare of the country and its inhabitants," and "to determine on some wise

153

and salutary measures" which should
bring up the Sound pirates with a round
turn. The Dutch representatives who
met them—members of the city government and of the Provincial Council—seeing their way to grinding some axes of
their own, recommended that a general
statement of grievances should be embodied, as usual, in a "remonstance"; and
that with the remonstrance, also as usual,
should be coupled a prayer for relief.
That method of procedure being agreed
to, an adjournment of a fortnight was
decided upon: to the end that the views
of the colonists of Long Island and of
Staten Island might be obtained more
fully, and that a larger number of delegates might be got together; in effect,
that the informal meeting might be raised
to the dignity of a little Landtag. Stuyvesant had no relish for such doings. The

action of the English, he declared, "smelt
of rebellion" and of "contempt of his
high authority and commission." But
the popular will was too strong for him
—or he was too weak to control it, which
amounted to the same thing — and he
"very reluctantly sanctioned the meeting that he could not prevent." Accordingly, on December 10th, with an aug-
mented membership, the council was re-
convened. Four Dutch towns and four
English towns were represented, and the
delegates—apparently chosen on a basis
of numerical representation — were ten
of Dutch and nine of English nativity.
And all of them, without regard to
nationality, harmoniously were agreed to
pool their grievances and to go for
Director Stuyvesant horns down!

Considering how serious those grievances were, the Remonstrance which

they formulated was couched in extraordinarily temperate terms. That document was drawn by one of the representatives from Gravesend, Ensign George Baxter—who is not to be confounded with the piratical Thomas—and as the work of an Englishman it is all the more remarkable for its tone of loyalty to the government of Holland. The preamble runs in these words: "Composed of various nations from different parts of the world, leaving at our own expense our country and countrymen, we voluntarily came under the protection of our sovereign High and Mighty Lords the States General, whom we acknowledge as our lieges; and being made members of one body, subjected ourselves, as in duty bound, to the general laws of the United Provinces, and all other new orders and ordinances which by virtue of the afore-

156

said authority may be published, agree-
ably to the customs freedoms grants and
privileges of the Netherlands."

What the remonstrants did object to,
and pointedly, was the publication of
new orders and ordinances which distinctly were disagreeable to the customs,
and still more disagreeable to the freedoms, of the home country. The first
and the main charge of their remonstrance was that such orders and ordinances had been enacted by the Director and Council "without the knowledge
or consent of the people," and that the
same were "contrary to the granted
privileges of the Netherland government, and odious to every free born man,
and especially so to those whom God
has placed under a free state in newly
settled lands, who are entitled to claim
laws not transcending, but resembling as

157

nearly as possible, those of the Netherlands."

Joined with this remonstrance in chief
—which, in effect, was no more than an
assertion of the fact that the colonists
were denied common right and common
justice—minor remonstrance was made
against the failure of the provincial government to protect persons and property; against the obligation to obey "old
orders and proclamations of the Director
and Council, made without the knowledge
or consent of the people," which "subject
them to loss and punishment through
ignorance"; against the "wrongful and
suspicious delay" in confirming land
patents; against land grants to favored
individuals "to the great injury of the
Province"; and against the appointment
of officers and magistrates "without the
consent or nomination of the people

. . . contrary to the laws of the Netherlands." In conclusion, the authors of
that surprisingly modest appeal added:
"As we have, for easier reference, reduced all our grievances to six heads, we
renew our allegiance, in the hope that
satisfaction will be granted to the country according to established justice, and
all dissensions be settled and allayed."

There is a very marked difference between the verbose and mean complainings of the more famous Remonstrance
of the year 1649 and the simple directness and dignity of this demand for
obvious rights; and had there been any
"established justice" for New Netherland — either in the provincial government or in the home government — it
could not have been met, as it was met,
by a flat refusal all around. Stuyvesant
made answer to it by a general denial,

that included a particular denial of the right of the delegates to assemble; and when the delegates replied, in turn, by an appeal to that natural law "which permits all men to assemble for the protection of their liberties and their property," he tersely ordered them to disperse "on pain of our highest displeasure"; to which lordly mandate, by way of a cracker, he added: "We derive our authority from God and the Company, not from a few ignorant subjects; and we alone can call the inhabitants together." In Holland, when the Remonstrance got there, the answer was the same. The Directors of the Company wrote to Stuyvesant (May 18, 1654) in these terms: "We are unable to discover in the whole Remonstrance one single point to justify complaint. . . . You ought to have acted with more vigor against the ringleaders

of the gang. . . . It is our express command that you punish what has occurred
as it deserves, so that others may be
deterred in future from following such
examples." And at the same time the
Directors wrote to the Burgomasters and
Schepens of New Amsterdam command-
ing "that you conduct yourselves quietly
and peaceably, submit yourselves to the
government placed over you, and in no
wise allow yourselves to hold particular
convention with the English or others
in matters of form and deliberation on
affairs of state, which do not appertain to
you; and, what is yet worse, attempt an
alteration in the state and its government."

The answer from Holland sustained one
half of Stuyvesant's declaration that he
derived his authority "from God and the
Company"—so far as the Company went,

his delegated authority was confirmed and sustained. But the other half of his declaration did not come out so well. A decade later his draft on divine power was returned dishonored; and only a turn of chance in his favor prevented that draft from going to protest within a year.

The twist of luck that saved him temporarily was the conclusion of peace (April, 1654) between England and Holland; and the consequent abandonment by Cromwell of his project for pacifying the colonial situation—in a breezily statesman-like fashion—by annexing New Netherland out of hand. Actually, the Protector's annexation scheme came to the very edge of being realized. An effective naval force was despatched from England; the New England colonies— Massachusetts alone lagging a little— buzzed with eager preparations for the fight that they so longed for; and the English colonists on Long Island, delightedly bustling to the front, made a fair start toward the impending revolution by declaring their independence of Dutch authority and by setting up a microscopic government of their own. And then, just as everybody (with the exception of Director Stuyvesant) was ready for things to happen, the peace was concluded—and nothing happened at all! But it was only by a very narrow margin that the orders for the seizure of New Netherland were countermanded before New Netherland was seized.

While the war was imminent New Amsterdam was in a whirl. Stuyvesant's mental attitude in the premises seems to have bordered upon consternation. In regard to practical provision for defence he wrote: "We have no gunners, no

musketeers, no sailors, and scarcely sixteen hundred pounds of powder"—a
statement that exhibits in rather a start-
ling fashion the physical unpreparedness
of the colony for a long-threatened war.
On its moral side the situation was worse.
The Director declared that he did not
expect "the people residing in the country, not even the Dutch," to back him
in the fight that was coming on; and
added: "The English, although they
have sworn allegiance, would take up
arms and join the enemy . . . to invite
them to aid us would be bringing the
Trojan horse within our walls."

By the Director's own showing, therefore, it appears that the spirit of loyalty
in the colony — if such a spirit can be
said ever to have existed—practically was
dead, and that the spirit of revolt was
very much alive. His English subjects

164

—almost openly in New Amsterdam, quite openly on Long Island—were impatient for the coming of their countrymen. His Dutch subjects were in a state of sulky mutiny that made them more than half ready to welcome the coming of anybody who would give them a new government of any sort—because of their moody conviction that any change whatever must give them a better government than that under which they lived. And it all was quite logical. It was the natural and inevitable outcome of thirty years of consistent misrule.

XVI

FOR my present purposes it is needless to treat at all in detail the last ten years of the Dutch domination of New Netherland. Little concessions continued to be made to the colonists; large wrongs continued to oppress them; there were more "remonstrances"; there was an Indian war. Fresh turns produced fresh figures in that small kaleidoscope, but the constituent elements of the figures remained unchanged. The essential change came from the outside; and even that was but the continued, yet always increasing, pressure of those forces which had begun to operate (as I have already written) before the unstable foundation

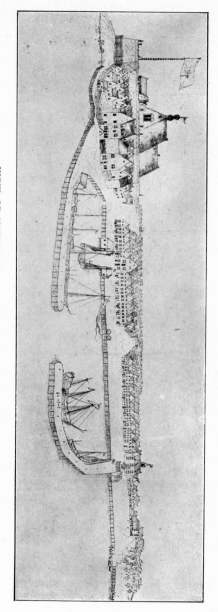

VIEW OF NEW YORK FROM BROOKLYN HEIGHTS, 1679

(From the Dankers and Sluyter drawing)

of the Dutch colony was laid. With the steadfast persistence of fate inevitable the English grip tightened as the English cordon closed in.

By the year 1659 the eastern end of Long Island—surrendered by Stuyvesant under the terms of the Treaty of Hartford (1650) — was a vigorous English colony; and was manifesting its vigor in a characteristic English fashion by crowding down into the Dutch territory westward of the Oyster Bay line. That thrust at close quarters was not easy to deal with. Releases of land were obtained in due form by Englishmen from accommodating sachems in temporary financial difficulties—or in chronic thirst that such transactions in real estate would provide means for temporarily slaking—and on the land thus obtained modest settlements were made. Presently, becoming immodest, the settlers of those settlements asserted that they were under the jurisdiction of Connecticut; an assertion that produced awkward conflicts of authority, no matter how hotly it was denied.

Up in the north, in the back-country, Massachusetts was reaching out to tap the Dutch fur-trade at its source: calmly ignoring the provisions of the Treaty of Hartford and claiming as her own all the territory between lines running westward from three miles south of the Charles and three miles north of the Merrimac straightaway across the continent to the Pacific. The southern line of that handsome claim of everything in sight down to sunset crossed the Hudson not far from Saugerties; and the kindly intention of the claimants was to relieve the Dutch of all care of the upper reaches of

the river, and incidentally to divert from
New Amsterdam to Boston the bulk of
the trade in furs. In presenting the
matter to Stuyvesant for consideration
(September 17, 1659) the Commissioners
shyly urged "we conceive the agreement
at Hartford, that the English should not
come within ten miles of Hudson's river,
doth not prejudice the rights of the
Massachusetts in the upland country, nor
give any rights to the Dutch there";
upon the strength of which ingenious
conception they asked that free passage
from the sea into and through the river
should be given to the English settlers—
"they demeaning themselves peaceably,
and paying such moderate duties as may
be expected in such cases"—resident
upon its upper banks. And by way of
justifying their modest request the Commissioners drew an airy parallel in free

169

international water-ways between the
Hudson on the one hand and on the
other the Elbe and the Rhine. It is
to Stuyvesant's credit that his reply
(October 29, 1659) to those cheeky Commissioners was a flat refusal; and that he
immediately sent off to the Amsterdam
Chamber—in order to be in a position
to back his refusal practically — a demand for "a frigate of sixteen guns."
That the frigate did not come was a mere
administrative detail quite in the natural
order of things.

By way of completing the English cordon, Lord Baltimore's people were pressing the Dutch from the south. The
Dutch trading - post on the Delaware
river—or the South river, as they called
it—was a losing venture from first to last;
and onward from the time (1638) of the
planting of the Swedish colony on the

west shore of the Delaware, on what nominally was Dutch territory, the government of New Netherland was involved in snarling difficulties in its efforts to maintain its rights. Before the Swedes were reduced to approximate order — even after their official conquest they continued to give trouble—the much more serious trouble with the English colonists of Maryland began.

Those complications were brought to a head by the formal demand (August 3, 1659) addressed by Governor Fendall, Lord Baltimore's representative, to "the pretended Governor of a people seated in Delaware Bay, within his Lordship's Province," to "depart forth of his Lordship's Province"—or to take the consequences! And Governor Fendall indicated what the consequences were likely to be by adding politely: "or otherwise

I desire you to hold me excused if I use
my utmost endeavour to reduce that part
of his Lordship's Province unto its due
obedience under him." The little ambassador who carried the Maryland governor's courteous but peremptory letter
to the Dutch commandant on the Delaware delivered it in a "pretty harsh and
bitter" manner; and emphasized its pur-
port by remarking incidentally that, "as
the tobacco is chiefly harvested," the
people of Maryland were quite at leisure
for a fight. "It now suits us," he concluded—in what no doubt was meant to
be a persuasive spirit—"best in the whole
year."

But the sporting offer of the Marylanders to fill in the close season for
tobacco with a time-killing war did not
materialize. Their ardor was a little
cooled, perhaps, by the prompt despatch

of reinforcements to the Delaware colony from New Amsterdam; and the assertion of possession was refuted so logically— on the ground that Lord Baltimore's patent gave him rights only to unseated lands, and therefore excluded him from a region colonized by the Dutch at least fifteen years before his patent was grant- ed—that for the moment their claim was shelved. It was by no means quieted, however. Until the Dutch were squeezed out and done for, the pressure of the English upon New Netherland from the south was continued with the same per- sistence that characterized the pressure of the English upon that unlucky colony from the east and from the north. There was no escape from those advancing ten- tacles: behind which, resistless, was the power of England. It was a cuttle-fish situation that could end in only one way.

173

The end would have come a trifle sooner, no doubt, had the Protector lived a little longer or had the Restora-ation followed directly upon his death. During the interval between September, 1658, and May, 1660, the domestic tribu-lations of the English gave them no time to bother about colonial extension: they had their hands full of matters requir-ing immediate attention at home. But when Charles II. resumed business as a king the would-be ousters of the Dutch in America instantly came to the front again.

Lord Baltimore was at the very head of the procession. "Charles had hardly reached Whitehall," as Mr. Brodhead puts it, "before Lord Baltimore instruct-ed Captain James Neale, his agent in Holland, to require of the West India Company to yield up to him the lands

174

on the south [west] side of Delaware Bay."
The Earl of Stirling, while less prompt
than Lord Baltimore, made up for his
seemly delay by an unseemly insistence.
In a petition to the King he set forth
that the "Councell for the affaires of
New England . . . in the eleaventh year
of the raigne of your Ma^{ts} royall Father
of blessed memory did graunt unto
William Earle of Sterlyne, your peti-
tioner's Grandfather, and his heires, part
of New England and an Island adja-
cent called Long Island. . . . That yor
Peticôners Grandfather and father, and
himselfe their heire, have respectively
enjoyed the same and have at their greate
costs planted many places on that Isl-
and; but of late divers Dutch have in-
truded on severall parts thereof, not ac-
knowledging themselves within your Ma^{ts}
allegiance, to your Ma^{ts} disherison and

your Peticôner's prejudice." Wherefore
he prayed: "May you^r Majestie be
pleased to confirme unto your Peticôner
his said inheritance to be held immediately of the Crowne of England, and
that in any future treaty betweene your
royall selfe and the Dutch such provision
may be as that the Dutch there may
submitt themselves to your Ma^{ts} gov-
ernem^t or depart those parts." Considering that the Stirling grant covered
Dutch territory, his lordship's neatest
turn is his reference to the intruding
"divers Dutch"; but there is an air of
easy assurance about his whole petition
that does credit to even a Scotch earl.

To Lord Baltimore's jaunty require-
ment, cited above, that the West India
Company should "yield up to him" the
lands on the west side of Delaware Bay,
the Directors gave "a proud answer": to

176

the effect that they "would use all the means which God and nature had given them to protect the inhabitants and preserve their possessions." But they manifested less pride, and more alarm, in a memorial that they promptly addressed to the States General: praying that a protest should be presented by the Dutch ambassador in London against English aggression; and that a demand should be made for the restoration to New Netherland of the territory that the English had "usurped." Under instructions from their High Mightinesses, the ambassador protested and demanded accordingly: and with precisely the same practical result that would have followed had he protested against the flowing of the tides, and had he demanded the cause of tidal eccentricities—the moon!

The Connecticut people, being keen to

assert what they were pleased to call their rights, followed close at Lord Stirling's aggressive heels. Governor Winthrop, on behalf of the General Court at Hartford, drew up (June 17, 1661) for the King's consideration a "loyal address": that wandered on lightly from expressions of loyalty to a specific request for a new charter by which his Majesty would assure them in possession of their territory against the Dutch—whom they affably described as "noxious neighbours," having "not so much as the copy of a patent" to the lands which they held. That there might be no room for a doubt as to what they wanted, they asked in set terms for a charter—calmly inclusive of the unpatented lands of their "noxious neighbours"—that should cover all the country "eastward of Plymouth line, northward to the limits of the Massachu-

178

setts colony, and westward to the Bay of Delaware, if it may be"; and that their modest petition might be presented properly and urged effectively they commissioned Governor Winthrop as their agent to carry it to England and to lay it before the King.

In those days passages across the Atlantic were taken where they offered. Actually, Winthrop went down to New Amsterdam—where he was given an "honourable and kind reception"—and sailed for England in the Dutch ship *De Trouw*. The Governor was not a dull man, and I think that he must have enjoyed, in the strict privacy of his inner consciousness, the subtle irony of the situation: as he courteously accepted his "honourable and kind reception" and then went sailing eastward under Dutch colors—and all the while having in his pocket that document which was meant to be a knife in the neck of his hosts at New Amsterdam and in the neck of the friendly power under whose flag he sailed. Had there been a Colonial Office in those days, and had Mr. Chamberlain been at the head of it, how he would have relished the story which that first colonial agent would have had to tell him when he got to land!

XVII

IN a way, the state of affairs in North
America in the year 1661 was very
like the state of affairs in South Africa
just before "Captain Jim" made his raid.
It all was on a smaller scale, of course, but
the facts and the conditions were much
the same. The Dutch were loosely seated in a valuable holding; their rule, arbitrary and corrupt, was resented muti-
nously by in-crowding greedy English
settlers who nominally were Dutch subjects; a belt of English colonies—more
complete than in South Africa—was
tightening about them; and at the back
of all the forces working for their destruction was the English government:

moved by the normal human desire to take possession of other people's valuable property; and more deeply moved by the instinctive feeling (which had no parallel in South Africa) that only by crushing the commerce of Holland could England become the leading commercial nation of the world.

It was against Dutch commerce that the blow was struck which led on quickly —and I think fortunately—to the extinction of the Dutch ownership of New Netherland. That blow was the revision, very soon after the Restoration, of the Navigation Act of 1651. As originally framed, the act had forbidden the importation of goods into England save in English ships or in ships belonging to the country in which the goods were produced. As amended, the act forbade, after December 1, 1660, the importation

182

or the exportation of goods into or from any of his Majesty's plantations or territories in Asia, Africa, or America save in English ships of which "the master and three fourths of the mariners at least are English."

This direct thrust at the commercial life of Holland was not lessened in force by the Convention agreed upon (September 14, 1662) between England and the United Provinces; rather, indeed, did the friction over that Convention tend to make matters worse. Mr. Brodhead, in his kindly way, asserts that "the Dutch fulfilled their stipulations with promptness and honor"; but, with all due deference to Mr. Brodhead, the Dutch did nothing of the sort—as the minutes of the Council for Foreign Plantations abundantly prove. On August 25, 1662, the Council ordered that "some heads of

183

remedies" should be drawn up to correct the abuses incident to "a secret trade driven by and with the Dutch for Tobacco of the growth of the English Plantations, to the defrauding His Matie of his Customs and contrary to the intent of the Act of Navigation." On June 24, 1663, the Council issued a circular letter to the governors of Virginia, Maryland, New England, and the West Indian Islands, drawing their attention to the "many neglects, or rather contempts, of his Maties commands for ye true observance" of the Navigation Act "through the dayly practices and designes sett on foote by trading into forrain parts . . . both by land and sea as well as unto ye Monadoes and other Plantations of ye Hollanders"; and in an undated document (Trade Papers lvii, 90) giving "certaine reasons to prove if the Duch

184

bee admitted trade in Virginia it wilbe greate loss to the Kings Matie and prejudice to the Plantacôn," the fact is stated that "there is now two shippes going from Zeland to trade there wch if they be admitted it wilbe losse to his Matie at least 4000^{li}, wch by your Lordshipps wisdome may be prevented."

All this, with more like it, goes to show that the "promptness and honor" of the Dutch in living up to the stipulations of the Convention left a little to be desired on the side of practicality; but it also goes to show — since two traders are necessary to a trade — that the English colonies took an active part in whistling the laws of their mother country down the wind. This secondary fact is brought out with clearness in a report (March 10, 1663) upon the South, or Delaware, river colony, which contains the pregnant as-

sertion: "Trade will come not only from
the City's colony but from the English;
who offer, if we will trade with them, to
make a little slit in the door, whereby we
can reach them overland without having recourse to the passage by sea, lest
trade with them may be forbidden by
the Kingdom of England, which will not
allow us that in their colony."

In this same report is the statement:
"The English afford us an instance of
the worthiness of New Netherland, which
from their Colony alone already sends
200 vessels, both large and small, to the
Islands"—an involved presentment of
fact that Mr. Brodhead misunderstands,
and in his restatement of it perverts into
meaning that the trade of New Netherland "with the West Indies and the
neighbouring English colonies now [1663]
employed two hundred vessels annually."

Obviously, the two hundred vessels referred to in the report hailed from English colonial ports; and they are cited to
show the "worthiness"—that is to say,
the fitness—of New Netherland to take
a larger share in the intercolonial trade.
But the essential fact is clear that the
many busy little ships then plying in
American waters, Dutch and English
alike, were snapping their top-sails at the
Navigation Act, and that a deal of illegal
trading was going on through that "little
slit in the door." Mr. Brodhead—in this
case with absolute correctness — summarizes the situation: "The possession
of New Netherland by the Dutch was, in
truth, the main obstacle to the enforcement of the restrictive colonial policy
of England." And the obstacles which
stood in the way of England's colonial
policy in those days—there is no very

marked change in these days—had to go down.

The final diplomatic round between England and Holland began in January 1664, when the Dutch ambassador in London was directed to insist upon a ratification by the British government of the long-pending Hartford Treaty; and so, by a definite settlement of the boundary question, clear the air. The answer to the Dutch demand certainly did settle the boundary question, and certainly did clear the air. It came two months later (March 12–22) in the shape of that epoch-making royal patent by which the King granted Long Island (released by the Earl of Stirling) and all the lands and rivers from the west side of the Connecticut to the east side of Delaware Bay to his brother, the Duke of York.

The actual conquest of New Nether-

LONGE

A DESCRIPTION OF THE
TOWNE OF MANNADOS
OR NEW AMSTERDAM

1664

This Scale of Fiue Hondred yeardes is For the Towne

"THE DU

(Photographed for this work from the original in the British

LAND.

Heads

Nut Ylaut

Heads

ye Gouernours House

Gouernours Garden

Hudſ

The MAINE.

(ing New Amsterdam in the year that it became New York)

land by the force sent out by the Duke
of York to take possession of his newly
acquired property, as I have written elsewhere, was "a mere bit of bellicose
etiquette: a polite changing of garrisons,
of fealty, and of flags"; and by way of
comment upon that easy shifting of
allegiance I farther have written in these
general terms: "Under the government
of the Dutch West India Company, the
New Netherland had been managed not
as a national dependency, but as a commercial venture which was expected to
bring in a handsome return. Much more
than the revenue necessary to maintain a
government was required of the colonists;
and at the same time the restrictions im-
posed upon private trade—to the end
that the trade of the Company might be
increased—were so onerous as materially
to diminish the earning power of the

individual, and correspondingly to make the burden of taxation the heavier to bear. Nor could there be between the colonists and the Company—as there could have been between the colonists and even a severe home government—a tie of loyalty. Indeed, the situation had become so strained under this commercial despotism that the inhabitants of New Amsterdam almost openly sided with the English when the formal demand for a surrender was made—and the town passed into British possession, and became New York, without the striking of a single blow."

XVIII

O N the side of ethics, the taking over
of New Netherland by the English
admits of differing opinions. Mr. Brodhead flat-footedly calls it "bold robbery."
Dr. Asher, himself a Dutchman, regards
it as the occupation by the English of
territory that was theirs by right of discovery, of settlement, and of specific
grant. For my own part—lacking the
temerity to pass judgment upon so vexed
a question—I am content to ignore the
ethical side of that easy conquest and to
ground my approval of it on the fact that,
as things then stood in Europe and in
America, it was the only practicable
treatment of an impossible problem; to

which, with submission, I add my conviction that for all the parties in interest
it was the best substitute for a solution
possible under the conditions which obtained.

The gain to England was so obvious
that it need not be discussed. The gain
to Holland was getting rid of a nettle of
a colony which—by involving her in an
outlay of more than a million guilders
above returns, and by most dangerously
complicating her relations with her most
powerful rival—from first to last did little
but sting her hands. The gain to the
English colonies in America was an immediate enlargement of intercolonial
trade: with a resultant solidarity of interests which strongly helped—a little
more than a century later—to bring about
their formal union and their definite independence. The gain to New Nether-

land—the essential matter here to be considered—was escape from a harsh and incompetent government, that crushed trade and that did much to make life unendurable, to the fostering care of a government that developed trade in every direction and that in its treatment of individuals erred on the side of laxness.

Out of that laxness came ill results. That the morals of New Amsterdam did not improve under English rule is not surprising—because New Amsterdam had no morals. On the other hand, its immorals—of which its supply was excessive—developed vigorously, in sympathy with its vigorously developing commercial life. In the last decade of the seventeenth century—what with our pirates and our slavers and the general disposition on the part of our leading citizens to

ride a hurdle race over all known laws,
including the Ten Commandments—New
York certainly was as vicious a little seafaring city as was to be found just then in
all Christendom. But the fact is to be
borne in mind that the evil state of affairs which developed under English government was put an end to by an English
governor. And the farther fact is to be
borne in mind that onward from the time
of that first reform governor there has
been in this town—as there conspicuous-
ly was not in this town during the Dutch
period of its history—at least an avowed
outward respect for decency and for law.
I do not assert, of course, that this ad-
mirable sentiment has shone brilliantly
or steadfastly, or that it is not badly
snowed under at times even now; but I
do assert that until we came under English rule such sentiment practically did

194

not exist at all. Lord Bellomont was the first of our governors—and this is not to cast a slight upon the excellent reorganizing work of Colonel Nicolls—who forced us to put some of our worst sins behind us, and so set us in the way (along which we still are floundering) to achieve that civic rectitude which was an unknown virtue in the Dutch times.

Having thus, for truth's sake, set forth the development and the curbing of our immorals which followed our taking on of a new nationality, I am free to make my final point — the enormous gain in material prosperity — in favor of that shifting of ownership which changed New Amsterdam into New York. When the English took over the city (September 8, 1664) the number of houses in it—as shown by Cortelyou's survey of the year

1660—was about 350, and the population was about 1500 souls. An authoritative record has been preserved—in the petition of the New York millers and merchants against the repeal of the Bolting Act— of exactly what this city gained in its first thirty years of English rule. The petition states that in the year 1678, when the Bolting Act became operative, the total number of houses in New York was 384; the total number of beef-cattle slaughtered was 400; the total number of sailing craft (3 ships, 7 boats, 8 sloops) was 18; and the total revenues of the city were less than £2000. The petition farther states that in the year 1694 (there is a secondary interest here, in that we see what the added two centuries have done for us) the number of houses had increased to 983; the number of beef-cattle slaughtered (largely for profitable export to the West Indies) to 4000; the number of sailing craft (60 ships, 40 boats, 25 sloops) to 125; and the city's revenues to £5000.

That statement of fact I conceive to be the most striking commentary that can be made upon the relative material merits of Dutch and of English rule. The sudden prodigious increase of the population and of the commerce of this city equally were due to a general easement of political and of commercial conditions: the first impossible while the Dutch domination continued; and the second rigorously withheld (of set purpose or of set stupidity) during the four decades that the West India Company betrayed all the interests of New Netherland in order to gain—yet failed to gain—its own selfish ends. I hope that we may

197

be able to make as good a showing in the Philippines at the end of our first thirty years.

But argument for or against that bold robbery, or that resumption of vested rights—as our two most authoritative historians, with a somewhat confusing divergence of opinion, respectively describe the English acquisition of New Netherland—no longer is necessary. As I have written, that once burning question became a dead issue in a time long past. Whatever were the equities of the conflicting Dutch and English claims to the most valuable slice of the continent of North America, they were quieted legally by the Treaty of Breda. And they have been quieted ethically—in the flowing of the years since that remote diplomatic agreement was executed—by

198

the passage of the property in dispute away from both claimant races into the possession of their descendants: who have coalesced into a new race, and who take their title from themselves.

INDEX

	PAGE
AFRICA, South, comparison with,	181
Alabama, Confederate cruiser,	32
Albany, lobbying at,	23, 39
"Strikes" at,	26
Antwerp, commerce of, destroyed,	33
Archangel, Russian port,	7
Armada, the,	64
Arms of Amsterdam, cargo of, 1626,	85
Arms of New York,	12, 58
Arms for Indians, Barent sells,	100
Confiscated,	99
Patroons sell,	69
Public sentiment about,	100
Trade in,	98
Van Rensselaer deals in,	99
West India Company responsible for,	101
Asher, life of Hudson by,	44
On collapse of West India Company,	119
On Count John Maurice,	115
On Dutch title to New Netherland,	42
On English conquest of N. Netherland,	191

201

INDEX

PAGE

BAHIA captured, 60
Baltimore, Lord, territorial claims of, 170, 174
Barent sells arms to Indians, 100
Barneveldt, execution of, 35, 44
    Opposes West India Company, 33
Baxter, George, drafts remonstrance, 1653, 156
    Leader of rebellion, 1655, 97
    Official interpreter, 95, 97
Baxter, Thomas, builds Wall St. palisadoes, 122
    Piracies of, 126
Beaver in civic arms, 58
Belgian refugees in Holland, 30, 33
Bellomont, Lord, character of, 110
    Reforms by, 195
Blake, Admiral, 122
Block, Adrien, commands *Tiger*, 13
    Discoveries of, 16
"Blood from King of Spain's heart," 63
Bogardus, daughter married, 81
Bolting Act, the, of 1698, 196
    Reference to, 59
"Bosch-lopers," 99
"Boss" and city charter synchronous, 142
Bout signs remonstrance, 1649, 76
Brazil, colony in, 115
    Conquests in, 60
    Evacuated, 1654, 118

INDEX

		PAGE
Breda, Treaty of,	44,	198
Bridgman, Orlando,		49
Brodhead, collector of documents,		2
On city charter,		140
On Dutch title to New Netherland,		42
On English conquest of N. Netherland,		191
Buzzard's Bay,		17

"CAPTAIN JIM'S" raid,		181
Carleton, Sir Dudley,		53
Chamberlain, Mr.,	53,	180
Charter, city, Brodhead on,		140
Granted to New Amsterdam, 1653,		139
Of liberties and exemptions, 1640,		94
Stuyvesant proclaims,		140
West India Company, granted, 1621,		45
Christiansen, Hendrick,		13
Church, dissatisfaction with,		80
Subscriptions to,		81
City Tavern built, 1642,		96
Civic rectitude unknown,		195
Coenties Slip,		96
Colonial discontent, nature of,		83
Commissioners of New England,		124
Congo Protectorate,	8,	72
Connecticut sends loyal address to King,		178
Territorial claims of,		178

INDEX

PAGE

Connecticut river (Fresh Water),   18
Convention of 1653,   151
   Frames remonstrance,   156
   How organized,   155
   Opposed by Stuyvesant,   154
Couwenhoven signs remonstrance, 1649,   76
Cromwell, death of,   174
   Plans annexation of New Netherland, 162
Custom-house, new,   13

DELAWARE RIVER, see South river,
De Vries, D. P., his opinion of the English,   89
   Honesty of,   73
   Stiffens Van Twiller's backbone,   89
Director General, official title of Governor,   70
"Door, little slit in the,"   186
Dutch colonists, characteristics of,   2, 9, 72
   Disloyalty of,   164
   "Noxious neighbours,"   178
Dutch somnolence a myth,   4, 9, 14, 27, 46
Dyck, H. van, on Van Tienhoven,   144
Dyer and Underhill, piracies of,   126

EAST INDIA COMPANY, purpose of,   47
Eendracht, case of the ship,   91
Elbertsen signs remonstrance, 1649,   76
England, peace with Holland, 1654,   162

INDEX

PAGE

England protests planting of N. Netherland, 53
  War with Holland, 1652, 122
English claim to New Netherland, 45
  Colonists call convention, 152
    Dissatisfied, 152
    Revolt of, 163
  Conquest of New Netherland, ethics of, 191
  Cordon around New Netherland, 167
  Grant covering New Netherland, 52
  In New Amsterdam, 1642, 95
  On Long Island rebel, 97
  Ship, first, in Hudson river, 88
    Refused trading license, 88
Exports from New Netherland, 85, 86
  From New York, 1678, 1694, 195

FENDALL, Gov., claims South river colony, 171
Feudalism in America, 68
"Figurative Map, the," 20, 41
Flushing, delegates from, 153
Fort Leavenworth, comparison with, 108
Fort, the, site of, 13
Fraunces's Tavern, 16
Fresh Water (Connecticut river), 18
Fur trade, Dutch, with Russia, 6
  At Manhattan, 8, 85
  Values of peltries, 86

INDEX

PAGE

GEORGE III., our feeling toward,   84
Gravesend, delegates from,   153

HAGUE, THE, lobbying at,   22, 39
Hall signs remonstrance, 1649,   76
Hardenburg signs remonstrance, 1649,   76
Hartford, Treaty of, granted too much,   132
    Ignored by Massachusetts,   168
    Ratification of, demanded,   188
Heermans, A., and Van Tienhoven,   148
    Signs remonstrance, 1649,   76
Hell Gate, *Onrust* goes through,   17
Hendricksen, Cornelis,   17, 19
Heyn, Admiral Peter,   61
Holland, peace with England, 1654,   162
    Political parties in,   34
    Protests against English aggression,   177
    Truce with Spain, 1609,   34
    War with England, 1652,   122
Hongers, Hans,   40
Hoogvelt, Lysbet van,   145
Houses in New York, 1664–78–94,   195
Hudson, Henry, death of,   6
    Discoveries of,   4
    Life of, by Asher,   44
    Report on fur trade by,   7
Hudson river called Mauritius,   13

INDEX

PAGE

Hudson river, Discovery of,   4
    Massachusetts claims passage of,   169

INDIAN war of 1643,   71
    Effects of,   103
Indians, arms sold to,   69, 98
    Land grants from,   167
    Sale of liquor to, forbidden,   109
Intercolonial trade, circa 1635, 1642,   88, 95
    Illicit,   184
Interpreter, official, 1642,   95
Irving, misrepresentations of,   1, 105, 132

JACOBSEN, C., commands the *Fortune*,   13
Jansen signs remonstrance, 1649,   76
Johannesberg,   72

KAMPEN, JOAN VAN,   135
Kieft, Wm., Director General, 1638–46,   70
    An ex-bankrupt,   70
    Arraigned in remonstrance of 1649,   79
    Church built by,   81
    Death of,   71
    Liberal government of,   95
    Portrait hung on gallows,   70
    Provokes Indian war,   71
    Steals ransom money,   71

INDEX

                                                    PAGE
Kieft welcomes refugees from N. England,   95
        Worst of all the Directors,   70
Kip signs remonstrance, 1649,   76
Kruger, President,   72

LAND grants from Indians,   167
        Unfairly made,   158
Liberties and exemptions, charter of,   94
Lobbying at The Hague,   22, 38
Long Island claimed by Lord Stirling,   175
        English on, 1659,   167
        Granted to Duke of York,   188
        Granted to Lord Stirling,   175
        Released by Lord Stirling,   188
Loockermans signs remonstrance, 1649,   76
Lothair, of Congo Protectorate,   72
Loyalty non-existent,   164

MANHATTAN ISLAND bought,   85
        Settlement on,   54
Manifest, first ship's,   86
"Map, the Figurative,"   20, 41
Maryland, trouble with,   171
Marylanders' sporting offer,   172
Massachusetts, pacific acts of, 127, 128, 129, 137
        Territorial claims of,   168
Maurice, Count John,   115

INDEX

	PAGE
Mauritius (Hudson) river,	13
May-day movings,	57
May, first Director General,	70
Milner, Sir Alfred,	53

NAHANT (Pye Bay),   17, 18
Narragansett Bay,   17
Navigation Act of 1651,   121
    Of 1660,   182
    Evasion of,   184
Negroes, permission to import,   133
New Amsterdam becomes New York,   190
    City charter granted, 1653,   139
    English in, 1642,   95
    First permanent colonists of, 57
    Founded,   50
    Immorals of,   193
    In war time, 1652,   122
    Named,   56
    Ordered to be made clean, 110
New England commissioners,   124
    Confederation, 1643,   124
    Desire in, to fight the Dutch, 125, 128, 162
    Early trade with New Netherland, 87, 90
New Netherland, an obstacle to England,   187
    Condition of, in 1624, 85
    Condition of, in 1629, 66

INDEX

PAGE

New Netherland, condition of, in 1647,   103
    Condition of, in 1649,   77, 108
    Condition of, in 1653,   157
    Condition of, in 1654,   163
    Condition of, circa 1660,   113
    Condition of, in 1661,   181
    Cromwell's plan for annexing,   162
    Dutch title to,   42
    Early trade with New England,   87, 90
    Easy conquest of,   186
    English claim to,   45, 52
    Erected into a province,   58
    Ethics of English conquest of,   191
    Exports from, 1624,   85
    Exports from, 1628–1635,   86
    First official use of name,   41
    Forces destructive to,   113, 120, 187
    Good results of English rule,   195
    Granted to Duke of York,   188
    Limits defined, 1616,   19
    Not named in W. I. Co. charter,   51
    Price of passage to, reduced,   133
    Population of, in 1629,   67
    Results of English conquest of,   192
    Unprepared for war, 1654,   163
    Company chartered,   40
        Directors of,   19

INDEX

	PAGE
New Netherland Company, members of,	40
Newtown, delegates from,	153
New York, arms of,	12, 58
Benefited by English rule,	195
Lawlessness of, 1690–1700,	193
Pirates,	193
Reformed by Lord Bellomont,	195
Statistics of, 1664, 1678, 1694,	195
Nicholas, Saint, patron of New York,	105
Onrust, yacht, built,	12, 13
Discoveries made in,	16, 19
Goes through Hell Gate,	17
Monument to,	15
Orange, House of, a rallying centre,	34
Oyster Bay line,	167
PASSAGE, price of, to N. Netherland reduced,	133
Patroons, grants to,	68
Relics of feudalism,	68
Sell arms to Indians,	69
Peace of 1654, Holland and England,	162
Pelgrom, Paulus,	19, 40
Pernambuco captured,	60
Petition of Lord Stirling to Charles II.,	175
Pilot who dared all for love,	91
Piracies on Long Island Sound, 126, 153,	154

211

INDEX

PAGE

Pirates of New York,   193

Placard encouraging discovery,   20, 21, 24

Planters' Plea, The,   66

Plymouth Company, grant to,   52

Population of New Netherland in 1629,   67

Pye Bay (Nahant),   17, 18

RAEF, SEBASTIEN, piracies of,   135

Rebellion on Long Island, 1655,   97

Refugees from Belgium,   30, 33

     From New England,   95

"Rehoboam, the crowning of,"   110

Remonstrance of 1649,   75

     Author of,   76

     On Stuyvesant,   105

     On Van Tienhoven,   143

     Signers of,   76

     Tone of,   81

Remonstrance of 1653,   155

     Author of,   156

     Rejected by West India Company,   160

     Resented by Stuyvesant,   160

     Tone of,   159

Remonstrances, various,   94, 166

Restoration, the,   174

Revenues of New York, 1678, 1694,   195

Rhode Island, disrepute of,   126

INDEX

Russia, Dutch trade with, PAGE 6

SALEM, teacher of church at, 128
Santiago, battle of, 64
Schout, duties of, 142
Ship *Arms of Amsterdam*, 85
    Eendracht, case of the, 91
    English, refused trading license, 88
    First, built on Manhattan, 11
    First English, in Hudson river, 88
    First trading, at Manhattan, 8
    Tiger burned, 13
Shipping of New York, 1678, 1694, 195
Ships, how built, 14
"Slate," the first, 141
Slave trade, beginning of, 133
"Slit in the door, little," 186
Smuggling, remonstrance 1649, 78
    Stuyvesant tries to check, 109
South river colony, 170
    Claimed by Maryland, 171, 172, 174
    Illicit trade with, 185
    Swedish colony on, 131, 170
Spain, colonial weakness of, 30
    King of, blood from heart of, 63
    Oppression of, 33
    Poor fighter at sea, 64

INDEX

	PAGE
Spain's truce with Holland, 1609,	34, 35
Ends, 1621,	44
Spanish colonies, trade with,	133
Sporting offer of Marylanders,	172
Stadt Huys built, 1642,	96
Convention of 1653 held in,	151
State rights, doctrine of,	129
States General, placard of 1614,	21
West India Company before,	37
Statute of Uses circumvented,	48
Stirling, Lord, claims Long Island,	175
Petition of,	175
Releases Long Island,	188
Stockton's "Great War Syndicate,"	32
Stuyvesant, Peter, Direc. Gen., 1647–64,	103
Bad domestic policy of,	137
Characteristics of,	105, 111
Charged with inciting Indian rising,	124
Concludes conventions with Virginia,	133
Derives his power "from God and the Company,"	160, 161
Fosters foreign trade,	136
Good foreign policy of,	124, 131, 136
Ineffective as a reformer,	111
Irving's caricature of,	105
Lays tax on wines and liquors,	110
Makes the first "slate,"	141

214

INDEX

	PAGE
Stuyvesant, P., opposes convention of 1653,	154
Orders town to be made clean,	110
Proclaims city charter,	140
Reduces Swedish colony,	131
Reforms attempted by,	109
Resents remonstrance of 1653,	160
Temporizing policy of,	98
Terms offered by, to New England,	125
Sunset, claim down to,	168
Swedish colony founded, 1638,	170
Reduced, 1655,	131

TAMMANY methods in 1653,	141, 150
Tavern, the City, built, 1642,	96
Tax laid on wines and liquors,	110
Tienhoven, Adriaen van, detected in fraud,	150
Cornelis van, character of,	143
Made schout,	142
Seduces Lysbet van Hoogvelt,	145
Tobacco, close season for,	172
Export tax on, removed,	133
Secret trade in,	184
Trade hampered, remonstrance 1649,	77
In 1624,	85
Intercolonial, circa 1635,	88
Circa 1642,	95
England objects to,	88, 90

INDEX

	PAGE
Trade, intercolonial, illicit,	184
Made easier, 1640,	94
Secret, in tobacco,	184
With drunken savages,	109
With Spanish colonies,	133
With West Indies,	197
Wrangles over the American,	27
Treasure fleet captured,	60
Treaty of Hartford granted too much,	132
Ignored by Massachusetts,	168
Ratification demanded,	188
Trojan Horse, the,	164
Tromp, Admiral van,	122
Truce, the twelve years',	34, 44
Tweenhuyzen, Lambrecht van,	19, 40

UNDERHILL and Dyer, piracies of,	126
United Colonies of New England, the,	124
Uses, statute of, circumvented,	48
Usselincx, William,	30

VAN CORTLANDT signs remonstrance, 1649,	76
Van der Douck drafts remonstrance, 1649,	76
Van Rensselaer deals in arms for Indians,	99
Van Twiller drives out English trading ship,	89
Verhulst, second Director General,	70
Virginia, conventions with,	133

216

INDEX

PAGE

Virginia, trade with,   88, 90, 133
Visscher, schipper,   123
Vries, see De Vries.

WALLOON colonists,   57
Wall Street palisadoes,   122
War between Holland and England, 1652,   122
    Indian, of 1643,   71
West India Company, the,   29
    Answer to Lord Baltimore,   176
    Arraigned, 1649,   77
    Before States General,   37
    Captures treasure fleet,   60
    Causes of its collapse,   114
    Chartered,   45
    Conquests in Brazil,   60
    Inquiry into affairs of, 1638,   94
    Memorial against English aggression, 177
    Naval strength of,   62
    No precedent for,   48
    Opposed by Barneveldt,   33
    Organized to make war,   47
    Rapacity of,   189
    Rejects remonstrance of 1653,   160
    Remonstrates against truce,   62
    Report on New Netherland, 1629, 60
    Rights and obligations of,   45

INDEX

PAGE

West India Co., selfish policy of, a failure, 197

    War winnings of, 61

    Writes to Burgomasters and Schepens, 161

West Indies, illicit trade with, 184

    Trade with, 88, 197

Windmill in the Fort, 80

Wines and liquors taxed, 110

Winthrop, Gov., drafts address to King, 178

    Goes in Dutch ship to England, 179

    Kindly received at New Amsterdam, 170

Witssen, Gerrit Jacob, 19

    Jonas, 19

Wooley, Charles, cited, 86

York, Duke of, grant to, 188

THE END